THE JURY PROCESS

...ng Scholar

...ago-Kent College of Law

TURNING POINT SERIES®

FOUNDATION PRESS
New York, New York
2005

THOMSON

™

WEST

Turning Point Series is a registered trademark used herein under license.

© 2005 By FOUNDATION PRESS

      395 Hudson Street
      New York, NY 10014
      Phone Toll Free 1–877–888–1330
      Fax (212) 367–6799
      fdpress.com

Printed in the United States of America

ISBN 1–58778–021–6

TEXT IS PRINTED ON 10% POST CONSUMER RECYCLED PAPER

TURNING POINT SERIES

CIVIL PROCEDURE

Civil Procedure: Class Actions by Linda S. Mullenix, University of Texas (Available 2006)

Civil Procedure: Economics of Civil Procedure by Robert G. Bone, Boston University (2003)

Civil Procedure: Preclusion in Civil Actions by David L. Shapiro, Harvard University (2001)

Civil Procedure: Territorial Jurisdiction and Venue by Kevin M. Clermont, Cornell (1999)

CONSTITUTIONAL LAW

Constitutional Law: The Commerce Clause by Dan T. Coenen, University of Georgia (2004)

Constitutional Law: Equal Protection by Louis M. Seidman, Georgetown University (2003)

Constitutional Law: The Religion Clauses by Daniel O. Conkle, Indiana University, Bloomington (2003)

CRIMINAL LAW

Criminal Law: Model Penal Code by Markus D. Dubber, State University of New York, Buffalo (2002)

FEDERAL COURTS

Federal Courts: Habeas Corpus by Larry W. Yackle, Boston University (2003)

FEDERAL COURTS

Federal Courts: Habeas Corpus by Larry W. Yackle, Boston University (2003)

INTERNATIONAL LAW

International Law: United States Foreign Relations Law by Phillip R. Trimble, UCLA (2002)

JURY AND TRIAL PRACTICE

The Jury Process by Nancy S. Marder, Chicago-Kent College of Law (2005)

LEGISLATION

Legislation: Statutory Interpretation: Twenty Questions by Kent R. Greenawalt, Columbia University (1999)

PROPERTY

Property: Takings by David Dana, Northwestern University and Thomas Merrill, Northwestern University (2002)

CORPORATE/SECURITIES

Securities Law: Insider Trading by Stephen Bainbridge, UCLA (1999)

TORTS

Torts: Proximate Cause by Joseph A. Page, Georgetown University (2003)

To my husband, Jeremy David Eden, who shares all my passions in life, including the study of the jury.

*

About the Author

Nancy S. Marder is a Professor of Law and Norman and Edna Freehling Scholar at Chicago-Kent College of Law. She is a graduate of Yale College, Cambridge University, and Yale Law School, where she was an Articles Editor of the Yale Law Journal. Professor Marder has clerked at every level of the federal court system, including a two-year clerkship with Justice John Paul Stevens at the U.S. Supreme Court, and one-year clerkships with Judge William A. Norris at the U.S. Court of Appeals for the Ninth Circuit and Judge Leonard B. Sand in the Southern District of New York. Professor Marder has written numerous articles on the jury that have appeared in law reviews such as Northwestern University Law Review, Texas Law Review, Iowa Law Review, and Southern California Law Review. She has presented her work on the jury at many conferences and symposia both in this country and abroad and regularly teaches a course on the jury entitled "Juries, Judges & Trials."

*

TABLE OF CONTENTS

TABLE OF CONTENTS

TABLE OF CONTENTS

THE JURY PROCESS

*

CHAPTER 1

AN INTRODUCTION: THE JURY PARADOX

The jury today presents a paradox. On the one hand, the jury is under attack in the popular press, in state legislatures, and by some judges. On the other hand, ordinary citizens who actually serve as jurors report positive feelings about the jury and their jury experience. In addition, national surveys show that the jury, as an institution, is held in high regard. Why are there two such contradictory, and often passionately held, views of the jury—so negative and so positive? Can they be reconciled, and if so, in what ways? If not, in what ways can and should the jury be reformed?

One way to begin to understand these two competing views is to recognize that the jury evokes strong responses in this country and that any assessment of the jury depends on from whose perspective the jury is being viewed. From the ordinary citizen's perspective, the jury provides one of the few opportunities, in addition to electoral voting, to participate directly in self-governance. Deciding a case is a first-hand lesson in democracy, even more so than voting, because the parties are present in the courtroom and the jury's verdict will directly affect them. Although many citizens seek to avoid jury duty initially, once they actually serve on a jury, a transformation occurs. They understand the enormity of their task, and perform it conscientiously, which may help to explain the positive feelings they have toward the jury after they have actually served on one.

In addition, at every stage of the jury selection and jury process, there are key features designed both to ensure that the jury system is fair and to convince ordinary citizens, whether they are jurors, parties, or members of the public, of its fairness. A *venire*, or panel of prospective jurors, is summoned from a fair cross-section of the community; they are questioned during *voir dire* in open court about their ability to serve; and they are struck from the *petit jury*, through the exercise of *for cause* or *peremptory challenges*, if they cannot be impartial or if they do not appear to be impartial. After the trial, the jury deliberates in secret, closed off from all those in the courtroom. The jury reaches a verdict, which in most criminal cases must be unanimous and in some civil cases can be by a majority, and this verdict is announced in open court. The individual jurors can then be polled to make sure that they are in agreement with the verdict.

Although each step of the jury process works reasonably well, no step is beyond improvement. The venire has sometimes failed to include members of minorities and other groups, thus raising the question: How should the venire be drawn so that it truly represents a fair cross-section of the community? Similarly, voir dire has not always elicited from prospective jurors all the information that the parties and their lawyers believe necessary and so questions such as the following arise: Can a balance be struck during voir dire so that prospective jurors provide relevant information to the parties without feeling that the questioning has been overly intrusive? Are there structural changes to the voir dire process that would allow this balance to be achieved? Peremptory challenges, which are supposed to provide parties with jurors whom they feel would be fair, have been abused by some lawyers, who, in their zeal to create a sympathetic jury for their clients, have succumbed to exercising peremptory challenges in a discriminatory manner. Such failings raise the following questions: Should the exercise of peremptory challenges continue, and if so, what safeguards should courts institute to preclude the exercise of discriminatory peremptories?

Another way to try to understand these two competing views toward the jury is to recognize that one's perspective is shaped by one's institutional role. Whereas ordinary citizens form their views based on their actual jury experience, other institutional actors will have other sources of information and other pressures shaping their views. For example, the press is likely to focus on issues of interest to their readers, and legislators are likely to focus on issues of import to their constituents. Perhaps, then, it is not surprising that the press has focused its coverage largely on verdicts in high-profile cases, on unusually high damage awards, and on juror bias. A number of state legislators have shared this concern. Legislators have debated whether damage awards should be capped, whether voting rules should be changed so that it is easier for criminal juries to convict, and whether certain types of civil matters should no longer be heard by juries. Even judges have entered this debate, agreeing with some in the press and legislature that damage awards are excessive or that certain types of cases should be removed from the jury's domain.

Finally, these various institutional actors—jurors, journalists, legislators, and judges—believe that improvements in the jury will come about in different ways. For the juror, and for that matter for many jury scholars, the problem is not with the jury but with the tools that jurors are given. If the jury is to perform its tasks more effectively, then jurors need to be given tools that will allow them to do so, whether these tools include instructions that are comprehensible, notepads and pens for note-taking, or the opportunity to submit written questions to the judge.

For some journalists, legislators, and judges, however, the way to improve jury performance is to limit the jury's responsibilities. They worry that the jury is not capable of deciding certain types of cases, such as those that are technical or complex. The response of some legislatures and judges has been to take such cases away from the jury and to give them to the judge. They also worry that juries are irresponsible in terms of damage awards. The response of some state legislatures has been to cap damage awards and the response of some judges has been to reduce jury damage awards. Fundamentally, some of these actors distrust the jury and see constraints on jury power as a way of limiting jury harm. Of course, legislatures, the judiciary, and the press are not monolithic; not all members of these institutions respond in the same way nor are they all guided by an underlying distrust of the jury.

By way of contrast, and in full disclosure, my own view is one of fundamental trust in the jury. When the jury falls short, which it does from time to time, like any institution, I think it reflects a failure on the part of courts or lawyers to provide jurors with adequate tools. My approach is to ascertain which tools jurors need to perform their job more effectively and to give them those tools rather than to limit their tasks.

Thus, my approach in this book will be to paint with broad brush strokes the roles the jury should serve (Chapter 2), as well as those roles it has served in the past and serves in the present (Chapters 3 and 4), before focusing on the institutional features of the jury, and which of those features work well today and which do not (Chapters 5, 6, and 8). The jury works in conjunction with the judge; the presence of a judge can inspire, educate, and constrain the jury, and that interaction needs to be examined (Chapters 7 and 9). Although I will address the popular criticisms raised by journalists, legislators, and judges, I do not think they have identified the areas most in need of jury reform, nor do I agree with their response to limit jury tasks (Chapter 10). Finally, I will turn to future directions our jury system can take, particularly with advances in technology, such as the Web (Chapter 11).

In sum, the goals of this book are: (1) to situate the jury in the rich legal tradition of which it is part; (2) to explain the defining features of today's jury; and (3) to identify those aspects of the jury where improvements can and should be made. The areas most in need of improvement, however, are not necessarily those that have been identified by the critics.

CHAPTER 2

AN OVERVIEW OF THE ROLES
OF THE JURY

The Jury's Fact-Finding Role

One well-known role of the jury is as fact-finder. In a jury trial, the judge will instruct the jury throughout the trial that the jury's job is to determine the facts of the case. The jury performs this job in part by observing the witnesses as they testify and assessing their credibility. In addition, the jury examines the exhibits that are offered into evidence and evaluates the arguments made by the attorneys. Throughout the trial, the judge also distinguishes between the judge's and jury's roles: the jury determines the facts, while the judge determines the law. Accordingly, the jury is supposed to take the law as the judge provides it. A common instruction to this effect is the following:

It will be your duty to decide from the evidence what the facts are. You will hear the evidence, decide what the facts are, and then apply those facts to the law which I will give to you. That is how you will reach your verdict. In doing so you must follow that law whether you agree with it or not.[1]

1. MANUAL OF MODERN CRIMINAL JURY INSTRUCTIONS FOR THE NINTH CIRCUIT, nos. 1.01 and 3.01 (1992).

The jury is particularly well suited for fact-finding. The jury consists of a group of individuals who work together to reach a group solution. Studies have shown that groups perform better than individuals in terms of solving problems and reaching correct answers.[2] Each member of the jury can contribute his or her recollection of the facts and evidence. Because different people remember different things, the jury has available for its consideration more information than a single individual might recall. Also, a group endeavor ensures that members of the jury can correct each other's mistaken ideas and faulty recollections. Each jury can consider how best to organize the material presented during the trial based upon different frameworks suggested by its members. The jury is well designed for fact-finding because its members can bring to the group deliberation different pieces of information and different frameworks by which to organize that information.

Although the judge highlights the principle that the jury's role is to find facts and the judge's role is to provide the law, the distinction is not always as clear cut as the judge would have the jury believe.[3]

2.   *See, e.g.*, Ballew v. Georgia, 435 U.S. 223, 233 n.15 (1978) (listing a study indicating that individual prejudice is more easily overcome in group situations and that larger groups are more effective in this respect than are smaller ones); REID HASTIE ET AL., INSIDE THE JURY 236 (1983) ("The group memory advantage over the typical or even the exceptional individual is one of the major determinants of the superiority of the jury as a legal decision mechanism.").

3.   *See, e.g.*, JEFFREY ABRAMSON, WE, THE JURY: THE JURY SYSTEM AND THE IDEAL OF DEMOCRACY 64 (1994) ("The fact/law distinction,

There are times that the jury, in the course of determining the facts, is also, in effect, interpreting and ultimately shaping the law.

For example, in a criminal trial, the judge instructs the jury that it must acquit the defendant unless the prosecutor has established the defendant's guilt "beyond a reasonable doubt." Although the judge has provided the jury with the legal standard of "beyond a reasonable doubt," that standard is vague and difficult to define. At best, the judge can tell jurors that there is no formula for deciding what constitutes "beyond a reasonable doubt," and that the jurors are to draw from their common sense and everyday experiences as to what it might mean. The jury must *interpret* that legal standard in deciding whether the prosecutor has met its burden in the defendant's case.

The jury's determination as to whether reasonable doubt has been met is based on more than finding the facts or applying the law. The jurors must engage in a weighing of the evidence presented by the State, and it is likely that this amorphous process of weighing and judging will be shaped by attitudes they hold on a wide range of issues, from whether they distrust the State and worry about it abusing its power to how vulnerable they feel to crime and whether they believe it is the State's responsibility to protect law-abiding citizens.

In a civil trial, the jury also engages in more than fact-finding, the judge's instruction notwithstand-

so starkly posed in judges' instructions to juries today, is, however, a fiction that seldom corrals the behavior of actual jurors.").

ing. For example, in negligence cases, juries must decide what behavior constitutes negligence. Although juries are instructed that the law requires "duty," "breach," "cause in fact," and "proximate cause," it is the jury's task to give meaning to these terms. Juries bring to these terms their sense of prevailing norms. With these standards in mind, jurors must decide whether to hold a defendant liable for the consequences of his conduct. In deciding whether there has been a breach, they must decide whether the defendant took reasonable care. The jury shapes the law in small, incremental ways each time it decides that someone did or did not take reasonable care in a particular case. Over time, a picture emerges as to what is meant by reasonable care.

The Jury's Political Roles

Buffer for the Defendant

The jury plays several political roles, one of which is to serve as a buffer between the criminal defendant and the government. In *Duncan v. Louisiana*,[4] Justice White described the criminal jury as providing a defendant "with an inestimable safeguard against the corrupt or overzealous prosecutor and against the compliant, biased, or eccentric judge."[5] The jury serves as a bulwark against government officials who exceed their authority. When officials in these other branches fail to perform their jobs properly, the jury interposes and ensures that the

4.   391 U.S. 145 (1968).

5.   *Id.* at 156.

criminal defendant does not suffer as a result of their overreaching.

Coordinate Branch of Government

The jury is a political actor in another sense as well: it not only protects the individual from government officials who overreach, but also it protects the citizenry from other branches' attempts to overreach. In our governmental scheme, there are three branches of government—the executive, legislature, and judiciary. The judiciary consists of both judges and juries. The jury is a coordinate branch of government, performing the political function of holding in check the other branches of government. The jury, drawn from the citizenry and serving for one case only, provides a counterbalance to the enormous power that judges, as unelected officials with lifetime tenure, wield.[6] The jury, as an integral part of the judiciary, helps to assuage fears about whether judges are too distant from ordinary citizens; the jury keeps judges in touch with ordinary citizens and their views of cases. The participation of juries also may help increase public acceptance of judicial decisions, even when the judicial decisions are unpopular.

Feedback to Other Branches

Yet another way in which the jury performs a political role is in its power to nullify, or to refuse to

6. Federal judges are appointed for life. In some states, judges are also appointed; however, in other states, they are elected. Even if elected, judges still wield enormous power. Although elected judges are beholden to voters, as a matter of practice, they are often difficult to unseat.

follow the law, in a given case. Although this is certainly a controversial view of the jury's proper role, and one with which most judges would disagree, one way to understand this role is to see the jury as providing feedback to the other branches of government every time it chooses to nullify. In some cases, the jury is saying to the legislature that it passed a law with which the jury disagrees; in other cases, the jury is saying to the executive that it has chosen to prosecute a case that the law was not intended to cover. Although the jury's message may be difficult to discern or susceptible to more than one interpretation in any given case, it will become clear as juries nullify over time in certain types of cases. According to this view, the jury's power to nullify is both a legitimate and essential mechanism for providing feedback to the other branches of government. It is only when nullification occurs too often (though how much is too much is open to great difference of opinion) that the system will falter.

Creating Political Awareness in Citizens

Yet another very different way in which "the jury is ... above all a political institution,"[7] as Alexis de Tocqueville described it over 170 years ago, is as a means of teaching citizens about the responsibilities of self-governance. In fact, Tocqueville wrote that he was not very sure how efficacious juries were as judicial decision-makers, but to his mind, this was not their key function; rather, they served the key

7. ALEXIS DE TOCQUEVILLE, DEMOCRACY IN AMERICA 272 (J.P. Mayer ed., 1969) (13th ed. 1850).

function of enabling citizens to participate in their democracy. He argued that civil juries, even more so than criminal juries, served this function because they "instill some of the habits of the judicial mind into every citizen, and just those habits are the very best way of preparing people to be free."[8]

Tocqueville thought that jurors would learn to think more judiciously from civil trials than from criminal ones because most citizens could imagine themselves embroiled in business disputes, but could not envision themselves ensnared in the criminal justice system. He also thought that jurors would take their cue more readily from the judge in civil cases, where they would look to the judge's expertise, than in criminal trials, where they would believe that they could understand the issues without needing to follow the judge's lead. In addition, in criminal cases, jurors would be wary about adopting the judge's views too uncritically because the judge was yet another arm of the government from which the defendant needed protection.

Badge of Citizenship

Finally, the jury serves a political function in that jury service is a badge of citizenship. For much of our history, jury service was limited to white men with property. Jury commissioners selected jurors from among those who satisfied these requirements and were regarded as moral and upstanding members of their community. African-American men and all women were categorically excluded from

8. *Id.* at 274.

jury service. For them, jury service became a symbol of their struggle for equality and full status as citizens. In light of a history of exclusion, it is not surprising that for African-American men and all women in particular, jury duty acquired political significance.

The Jury's Educational Roles

Lessons in Democracy

The jury's educational roles are tied closely to several of its political roles. One of its educational roles, which in Tocqueville's view is the main function of the jury, is to educate citizens about the responsibilities of democracy. Tocqueville viewed the jury as a "free school,"[9] teaching citizens about self-governance. Jury service and electoral voting are the two ways that citizens in a democracy participate in their government, and jury duty in particular enables citizens to participate directly. They see the parties in the courtroom and know that the jury verdict will have consequences for them. Now that many states have reduced the number of exemptions, which automatically exclude certain categories of people from jury service, more of the populace is available to serve as jurors and to learn about the legal system from this firsthand experience.

Jury duty also teaches more subtle lessons about citizenship—about who counts and who does not. When African-American men and all women were denied the opportunity to serve on juries, the lesson

9. *Id.* at 275.

they learned was that they were not full citizens. In contrast, white men with property, who were given the opportunity to serve, learned the lessons that they were full citizens, and concomitantly, that all others were not.

Lessons in Diversity

Today, jury service provides another educational function: it brings together people from all walks of life and has them work together. Jury service provides one of those rare settings, even more so than the military and public school, where people of different races, ethnicities, genders, ages, classes, religions, and sexual orientations, are summoned to appear and to accomplish a discrete task. For some jurors, this might be the only time they have worked with such a diverse group of people. Jury duty, then, provides jurors with a unique opportunity to view a case through many different lenses. It also provides jurors with a unique challenge: after they have viewed the case from so many different perspectives they must reach one point of view so that they can render a verdict.

Jury duty not only educates those who serve as to the challenges and benefits of engaging in problem-solving with a diverse group of participants, but also it educates society-at-large as to the importance of diversity in a work environment. Today, there is an expectation that juries will be diverse, and, to the extent they are not, those who belong to groups that have been excluded question whether to accept the verdict. Although the Supreme Court has interpreted the Sixth Amendment to require only that the venire, and not the petit jury, be drawn from a fair cross-section of the community,[10] there is nevertheless an expectation that juries will be diverse. When juries lack diversity, they not only lose the benefit of different jurors offering different perspectives during deliberations, but also they raise various spectres, such as jury manipulation or exclusivity, that impugn the integrity of the jury system.

Lessons in New Technologies

Finally, today's jury has the potential to educate jurors on the new tools of a democracy. Although courts have been slow to embrace technology, once they do, they can provide jurors with an education in the use of these new tools. For example, some courts have begun to use the Internet to summon prospective jurors for jury duty, to communicate about excuses, deferrals, and hardships, and to provide general juror orientation that has traditionally been done only in the courthouse. Courts could go much further in using technology to make jury duty more convenient and efficient. For example, they could permit prospective jurors to complete supplementary written questionnaires on the Internet rather than in the Jury Assembly Room and to allow basic information that is typically elicited during voir dire in the courtroom to be gathered by

10. *See* Holland v. Illinois, 493 U.S. 474 (1990) (holding that the Sixth Amendment's fair cross-section requirement of the venire need not be applied to the petit jury); Batson v. Kentucky, 476 U.S. 79, 85 n.6 (1986) ("[I]t would be impossible to apply a concept of proportional representation to the petit jury in view of the heterogeneous nature of our society.").

"Web voir dire" on the computer. Were courts to make good use of technology, not only would they improve the jury experience, but also they would educate some prospective jurors as to these new forms of communication. Again, the jury, in addition to the public school system, could help to bridge some of the "digital divides" that separate those who are familiar with these new technologies from those who are not. The jury could serve as this educational bridge by introducing prospective jurors to these new technologies and helping them to feel comfortable with them in the course of their jury duty.

CHAPTER 3

A BRIEF HISTORY OF THE JURY

The Medieval Jury: Investigative Jurors

Although the jury is an institution of ancient lineage, there are several ways in which the medieval jury, the precursor to our modern-day jury, varied significantly. Perhaps one of the most striking differences is that medieval jurors were chosen as jurors because they were familiar with the parties and the facts of the dispute. They were selected *because of* their knowledge. If they did not have sufficient familiarity with the dispute, they were expected to seek out additional jurors who did. This is in stark contrast to today's jurors who are chosen because they have no personal knowledge of the parties or the dispute. Whereas the medieval jury relied on jurors who were already informed, today's jury relies on jurors who are uninformed, and who become informed only from the evidence and arguments presented at trial.

One reason for the medieval jury's reliance on informed or "self-informing"[1] jurors was that the jury performed its fact-finding function outside of the supervision of the court. Fact-finding was a

1. THOMAS ANDREW GREEN, VERDICT ACCORDING TO CONSCIENCE: PERSPECTIVES ON THE ENGLISH CRIMINAL TRIAL JURY 1200–1800, at 16 (1985).

cumbersome, expensive process. By leaving it to the jurors to perform on their own, the British Crown spared itself the administrative expense of fact-finding. By assigning fact-finding to jurors rather than to Crown-appointed judges, the British Crown protected its judges from the dissatisfaction that might otherwise be directed toward them by the losing litigant.

Another significant difference between the medieval juror and today's juror is that the former played an active, independent role in fact-finding, whereas the latter remains passive and depends on others to present testimony and exhibits from which the juror is to decide the facts. Medieval jurors, charged with fact-finding, performed this task without any supervision or assistance from the court. Their investigations might have taken them out into the community, where they could interview neighbors who had information to contribute. In contrast, today's jurors are supposed to enter the courtroom without any preconceived notions about the case. The only evidence they are supposed to use in their decision-making is that which is presented to them in the courtroom by the lawyers and permitted by the judge.

Medieval jurors' independent fact-finding meant that they had information that the court did not have; thus, it was more difficult for judges to second-guess the jury's factual determinations. In contrast, today's judge hears what the jury hears, and if the judge thinks that a reasonable jury could not have reached the verdict that the jury reached, there are procedural devices that allow the judge to take the case away from the jury. Although the factual findings of today's jury are entitled to deference, the trial judge, present in the courtroom, can still weigh in with his or her judgment as to whether the moving party (or the government) has met its burden. The medieval jury's independent fact-finding meant that its factual determinations were outside of the judge's realm, and therefore, it exercised a degree of authority that today's jury does not have.

Medieval jurors' independent investigation of the facts meant that they could use this capacity to circumvent an unduly harsh penalty. For example, the penalty for felony murder was death. Medieval juries resisted this penalty in some cases by finding facts to be such that the felony murder criteria were not met even in cases when they clearly were. Through their power to investigate the facts independently, medieval juries were able to resist a rigid legal regime until the government eventually recognized degrees of homicide and established less drastic penalties.

The American Colonial Jury: Finding Facts and Law

The jury, when transplanted to American soil, no longer performed investigative fact-finding outside of the courtroom; however, inside the courtroom, it engaged in both fact-finding and interpretation of the law. Judges typically instructed jurors that they were free to decide the facts and the law.[2] In addition, judges informed jurors that the decision they reached should be consistent with their sense of what was right. John Adams expressed this view when he described the juror's duties as follows: "It is not only his right but his duty, in that case to find the verdict according to his own best understanding, judgment, and conscience, though in direct opposition to the direction of the court."[3]

Even if judges had tried to instruct jurors on the law, there are several reasons why the instructions might have been difficult to follow. According to one study of the legal system in Massachusetts before the Revolutionary War,[4] judges' instructions could be confusing because they were delivered seriatim by at least three judges, and so it would be difficult for jurors to know which instructions to follow if the judges differed in their approaches. To further confuse matters, lawyers had the opportunity to present their own instructions on the law. Moreover, even if the judges' instructions were consistent with each other and clear, judges had few devices available to them to compel jurors to follow their instructions. Between judge and jury, the jury exercised the greater power, with the judge largely

2. *See, e.g.,* Mark DeWolfe Howe, *Juries as Judges of Criminal Law*, 52 HARV. L. REV. 582, 589, 595 (1939).

3. *Id.* at 605 (quoting 2 LIFE AND WORKS OF JOHN ADAMS 253–55 (C.F. Adams ed., 1856)).

4. *See* WILLIAM E. NELSON, AMERICANIZATION OF THE COMMON LAW: THE IMPACT OF LEGAL CHANGE ON MASSACHUSETTS SOCIETY, 1760–1830, at 26–27 (1975).

serving as a means of keeping order in the courtroom.[5]

There is some debate among commentators about
when the balance of power shifted and the jury lost
its explicit right to decide the law, but most seem to
agree that the jury maintained this right until at
least the 1850s.[6] Commentators have pointed to
various state constitutions and state supreme court
decisions that took the position that the jury was to
judge the law as well as the facts. In some states,
the legislature had passed statutes that explicitly
provided that juries were to be the finders of fact
and law. Even with such laws on the books, however, judges in these states, such as Louisiana, Connecticut, Massachusetts, Illinois, and Georgia, began to wrest this power from the jury in the late
1800s.[7]

Transformation to the Modern-Day Jury

There are various accounts of how the jury
evolved from a body that was authorized to decide
both law and facts up until the mid–1800s to one

5. *See* Howe, *supra* note 2, at 591 ("The judges in Rhode
Island held office not for the purpose of deciding cases, for the
jury decided all questions of law and fact; but merely to preserve
order, and see that the parties had a fair chance with the jury.")
(quotation omitted).

6. *See, e.g.*, Alan W. Scheflin, *Jury Nullification: The Right
To Say No*, 45 S. Cal. L. Rev. 168, 177 (1972) ("There is
agreement among many commentators that the right of the jury
to decide questions of law and fact prevailed in this country until
the middle 1800's.").

7. *See* Howe, *supra* note 2, at 597 n.58, 602–03, 609–10, 611,
616.

whose sole responsibility, at least according to the judge, is to decide the facts and apply the law as given to it by the judge.

One broad-brush picture of the transformation from medieval to modern-day jury is provided in an article by Professor Stephen Yeazell.[8] He explained that the move from independent fact-finding jurors to jurors who rely on in-court presentations for their fact-finding meant that courts needed rules to govern the presentations. With the development of rules of evidence, both lawyers and judges had larger roles to play. Lawyers assumed responsibility for presenting their respective versions of the facts, and judges exercised control over the lawyers' presentations, and over the verdicts that were supposed to be based on those presentations. As the judges' and lawyers' roles expanded, the jurors' roles contracted. Jurors depended upon lawyers for the presentation of the facts and upon judges for instructions on the law. They were constrained in ways that their medieval predecessors had not been: they were selected for their ignorance of the facts and parties; they were made to rely on the lawyers' presentations of the facts; they were dependent on the judge for an explanation of the law; and they were expected to reach a verdict based on what they had seen and heard in the courtroom, with the added threat that the judge could order a new trial

8. Stephen C. Yeazell, *The New Jury and the Ancient Jury Conflict*, 1990 U. CHI. LEGAL F. 87.

or take the case away from the jury if the verdict did not comport with the evidence. In the modern-day courtroom, lawyers have gained control over the presentations and judges have gained control over the trial proceedings; all that remained for jurors was to sit back and listen.

Other explanations for why judges acquired more power in the courtroom, at the expense of juries, were that there was a growing faith in judges to protect the rights of criminal defendants[9] and there was a changing role for judges once lawyers had to present their cases in court and judges had to make evidentiary rulings.[10] In colonial times, juries were seen as the best protection a criminal defendant could have from the government. This was especially true when judges were appointed by the British Crown. There was a perception that judges would feel that their allegiance was to the Crown, which paid their salaries, and that judges who sat in England would be unfamiliar with conditions in the colonies.[11] In addition, judges during this period were laypersons, not lawyers, so there was a question why they should command any more authority in the courtroom than any other layperson, such as a juror. Eventually, however, judges were drawn from those who had legal training. Therefore, they had specialized knowledge that jurors did not have. When judges emerged from a professional class and

9. ABRAMSON, *supra* note 3 (Ch. 2), at 87–90.

10. Yeazell, *supra* note 8, at 94–96.

11. *See* Duncan v. Louisiana, 391 U.S. 145, 152 (1968) ("The First Continental Congress, in the resolve of October 14, 1774, objected to trials before judges dependent upon the Crown alone for their salaries and to trials in England for alleged crimes committed in the colonies....").

were no longer appointed by the Crown, the distrust that the populace once had for them abated.

Yet another explanation for the growing power of the judge and the diminishing role of the jury, which I offer as speculation, is that this transformation corresponds to a change in the potential membership of the jury.[12] In the late 1800s, at the same time as judges were taking law-making powers away from juries, juries were beginning to include African-American men and some women (depending upon the state). With the passage of the Fifteenth Amendment in 1870,[13] African-American men had acquired the right to vote, and with it, the right to serve on juries. Some states responded by passing statutes that barred African-American men from jury service, but these were eventually declared unconstitutional by the Supreme Court in 1880.[14] Although court officials[15] and lawyers[16] had other devices to prevent African-American men, and later

12. *See infra* text accompanying notes 17–28 (describing more fully the change in who could serve as a juror).

13. The Fifteenth Amendment provides in relevant part: "The right of citizens of the United States to vote shall not be denied or abridged by the United States or by any State on account of race, color, or previous condition of servitude." U.S. CONST. amend. XV, § 1.

14. *See* Strauder v. West Virginia, 100 U.S. 303 (1880).

15. *See* Nancy S. Marder, *The Myth of the Nullifying Jury*, 93 Nw. U. L. REV. 877, 888 n.42 (1999) (citing state court cases in which court officials kept African-American men from serving on juries by failing to include their names on lists from which venires were drawn).

16. *See infra* text accompanying notes 66–90 (Ch. 5)(describing the use of discriminatory peremptory challenges).

women, from actually being seated on juries, judges were another means of controlling the new jury. If African-American men and women could not be kept off the jury entirely, then the jury's role could at least be limited by the judge.

Structural Changes in the Modern-Day Jury

If the modern-day jury can be said to have come into existence in the mid–1800s as judges began to wrest law-making powers from juries, it is remarkable how few structural changes the jury as an institution has undergone since that time. Among the most significant structural changes are an expansion in terms of who can serve as jurors, a reduction in the size of the civil jury, and a recent, though still fairly limited, effort to restore jurors to a more active role.

Opening Up Jury Service

At the founding of this nation, jury duty was one of the responsibilities of citizenship, and those who were citizens could serve on juries. At the time, citizens were white men with property. From this group, Jury Commissioners selected for jury service those with reputations as upstanding members of the community.

For African-American men and all women, the quest for jury service was an arduous one, with many impediments placed in the way. Even when African-American men and all women were allowed to vote,[17] which was one badge of citizenship, they

17. The Fifteenth Amendment, enacted in 1870, gave African-American men the right to vote. See *supra* note 13. Fifty

were not always permitted to serve as jurors, which was the other badge of citizenship. In *Strauder v. West Virginia*,[18] the U.S. Supreme Court held that state statutes such as the one in West Virginia, which prohibited African-American men, but not white men, from serving as jurors, violated the Equal Protection Clause of the Fourteenth Amendment. After *Strauder*, such statutes were impermissible. However, even when these statutes were removed from the books, African-American men were kept from serving on juries through other devices. Lawyers used peremptory challenges, for which no explanation was necessary, to strike African-American men from the venire. The practice was alleged in *Swain v. Alabama*,[19] and persisted for at least the next twenty-five years, until the Supreme Court decided *Batson v. Kentucky*.[20] However, even after *Batson*, in which the Supreme Court created a modified peremptory challenge so that reasons must now be given if race is suspected as the basis for the peremptory, peremptories still can be used to remove African Americans from the jury by lawyers who are of a mind to discriminate.[21]

years later, in 1920, the Nineteenth Amendment gave all women the right to vote: "The right of citizens of the United States to vote shall not be denied or abridged by the United States or by any State on account of sex." U.S. CONST. amend. XIX.

18. 100 U.S. 303 (1880).

19. 380 U.S. 202 (1965).

20. 476 U.S. 79 (1986).

21. After *Purkett v. Elem*, 514 U.S. 765 (1995) (*per curiam*), a lawyer's reason for exercising a peremptory challenge can be unrelated to the facts of the case. The reason can be "implausi-

The opportunity to serve on a jury came about even more slowly for women than for African-American men. Women were permitted to serve on juries in federal and state courts only in states that permitted women to serve; the federal courts took their cue from the state courts. The first state to permit women to serve, albeit sporadically, was Wyoming, under its 1869 Act to Grant to the Women of Wyoming Territory the Right of Suffrage, and to Hold Office.[22] Utah, which allowed women to serve as jurors in 1898, has traditionally been credited as the first state to allow women jurors,[23] perhaps because they were permitted on a more widespread basis than in Wyoming. It was not until the Civil Rights Act of 1957[24] that the federal courts no longer depended upon state court practices.[25] Yet, even when women could technically serve on juries, states used the practice of affirmative registration— requiring women to register to serve if they wanted

ble or fantastic" or "silly or superstitious," *id.* at 768, as long as it is nondiscriminatory. However, the Court, by giving lawyers such leeway, has further weakened *Batson* and has allowed the peremptory, once again, to function as a vehicle for discrimination.

22. *See* Carol Weisbrod, *Images of the Woman Juror*, 9 HARV. WOMEN'S L.J. 59 n.2 (1986).

23. *See id.*

24. Pub. L. No. 85–315, § 152, 71 Stat. 634, 638 (codified as amended at 28 U.S.C. § 1861).

25. Hoyt v. Florida, 368 U.S. 57, 60 n.2 (1961) ("From the First Judiciary Act of 1789 to the Civil Rights Act of 1957—a period of 168 years—the inclusion or exclusion of women on federal juries depended upon whether they were eligible for jury service under the law of the State where the federal tribunal sat.") (citations omitted).

to be called for jury service, but not making the same demand of men—to limit women's partic- ipation so that they would not be taken away from their duties at home.[26] Finally, in 1975, the Su- preme Court held in *Taylor v. Louisiana*[27] that the systematic exclusion of women through affirmative registration violated a defendant's Sixth Amend- ment right to a jury venire drawn from a fair cross- section of the community. Even after *Taylor*, how- ever, women could still be prevented from being seated on a jury through an attorney's exercise of gender-based peremptory challenges. More recently, the Supreme Court held in *J.E.B. v. Alabama ex rel. T.B.*[28] that peremptories cannot be exercised on the basis of gender.

Reducing the Size of the Civil Jury

In the 1970s, there was another significant struc- tural change in the modern-day civil jury—a reduc- tion in its size. Although federal criminal juries typically consist of twelve jurors,[29] as do many state criminal juries,[30] federal civil juries today can have

26. *See id.* at 57 (holding that Florida's practice of affirma- tive registration for women but not for men did not violate the defendant's Fourteenth Amendment right to due process).

27. 419 U.S. 522 (1975).

28. 511 U.S. 127 (1994).

29. *See* FED. R. CRIM. P. 23(b) ("Juries shall be of 12 but ... the parties may stipulate in writing with the approval of the court that the jury shall consist of any number less than 12 or that a valid verdict may be returned by a jury of less than 12 should the court find it necessary to excuse one or more jurors for any cause after trial commences.").

30. The number of jurors on a criminal jury in state court is typically twelve, but cannot go below six jurors. *See* Ballew v.

from six to twelve jurors,[31] as do most state civil juries, and in practice, most federal and state civil juries consist of six to eight jurors.

The move to reduce the size of the civil jury in the 1970s sparked much debate among academics, lawyers, and judges. As federal and state judges experimented with smaller civil juries, the debate raged on; eventually, it abated after the Supreme Court held that there was nothing magical about the number twelve and that civil and criminal jury trials of at least six jurors were consistent with the Sixth[32] and Seventh Amendments;[33] however, juries of fewer than six jurors would run afoul of the Fourteenth Amendment.[34] Many judges and lawyers favored the reduction in jury size because they believed it would be cost-effective, efficient, and just. However, many academics opposed the reduction because they thought it would limit the range of perspectives available to the jury, produce less representative juries, and result in less consistent verdicts from jury to jury.[35] Today, it is fairly commonplace for civil juries to consist of six to eight jurors, and this practice enjoys the support of many judges[36] and lawyers, though not all academics.[37]

Georgia, 435 U.S. 223, 232–38 (1978) (holding that a jury in a state criminal trial cannot go below six jurors).

31. *See* Fed. R. Civ. P. 48 ("The court shall seat a jury of not fewer than six members and not more than twelve members. . . .").

32. Williams v. Florida, 399 U.S. 78, 86–102 (1970).

33. *See* Colgrove v. Battin, 413 U.S. 149, 160 (1973) (holding that a civil jury of six members did not violate the Seventh Amendment right to a jury trial).

34. *See* Ballew v. Georgia, 435 U.S. 223 (1978).

35. *See, e.g.,* Richard Lempert, *Uncovering "Nondiscernible" Differences: Empirical Research and the Jury-Size Cases,* 73

Encouraging Active Jurors

The most recent procedural changes in the jury are the result of an effort to encourage jurors to be active participants throughout the trial process. This effort has been spearheaded by a number of state court judges. One proponent of jury reform, and of the model of active jurors, is now-retired Arizona Superior Court Judge B. Michael Dann. He observed that in most courtrooms, jurors are supposed to sit passively throughout the trial; it is assumed that they will simply absorb the information presented. They are not to take an active role until they begin their deliberations, even if the trial has lasted for weeks or months.

In an effort to transform jurors from passive observers to active participants,[38] Judge Dann and the other members of the committee for jury reform in Arizona proposed a number of sweeping changes

MICH. L. REV. 643 (1975); Hans Zeisel & Shari Diamond, *"Convincing Empirical Evidence" on the Six Member Jury*, 41 U. CHI. L. REV. 281 (1974).

36. *See, e.g.*, Improving Jury Selection and Juror Comprehension, Workshop co-sponsored by the Federal Judicial Center and the Institute of Judicial Administration at New York University School of Law (Dec. 13, 1996) [hereinafter Improving Jury Selection and Juror Comprehension] (notes on file with author).

37. *See, e.g.*, Shari Seidman Diamond et al., *Juror Judgments About Liability and Damages: Sources of Variability and Ways to Increase Consistency*, 48 DEPAUL L. REV. 301, 317 (1998) (proposing a return to the twelve-person civil jury to reduce variability in jury damage awards); Nancy S. Marder, *Juries and Damages: A Commentary*, 48 DEPAUL L. REV. 427, 446 (1998).

38. *See, e.g.*, B. Michael Dann, *"Learning Lessons" and "Speaking Rights": Creating Educated and Democratic Juries,*

to jury procedures.[39] These reforms included: providing jurors with a list of exhibits, witnesses, and
other useful information at the start of the trial,
instructing jurors about the case both at the beginning and at the close of the trial, permitting jurors
to take notes and to submit written questions to the
judge during the trial, allowing jurors to discuss the
case during the trial, and having the judge engage
in a dialogue with the jury should it reach an
impasse to determine whether it would be helpful to
have the lawyers provide additional arguments.[40]
Arizona judges agreed to adopt many of these reforms,[41] albeit some on a temporary basis and limited to civil jury trials, and have opened their courtrooms to researchers who are evaluating how well
these procedural changes are working.[42]

68 IND. L.J. 1229, 1241 (1998) ("Relying on the evidence produced by scientific studies and having as their goals better-
informed jurors and more accurate verdicts, social scientists, law
professors, a few judges, and others paint a far different picture
of jurors and advocate a far different model for the jury than the
one now followed in most courtrooms in this country. They all
agree on one thing: jurors must be permitted to become more
active in the trial.").

39. *See* THE ARIZ. SUPREME COURT COMM. ON MORE EFFECTIVE USE
OF JURIES, JURORS: THE POWER OF 12 (1994) [hereinafter THE POWER
OF 12].

40. *Id.* at 19–28.

41. *See, e.g.*, William H. Carlile, *Arizona Jury Reforms Buck
Legal Traditions*, CHRISTIAN SCI. MONITOR, Feb. 22, 1996, at 1
(reporting that Arizona adopted eighteen of the jury reform
panel's fifty-five recommendations).

42. *See generally* Paula L. Hannaford et al., *Permitting Jury
Discussions During Trial: Impact of the Arizona Reform*, 24 LAW

One impetus for these reforms was a view that the conventional role of the juror as a passive receptacle into which information could simply be poured was contrary to how people actually learn.[43] The Arizona judges understood that jurors could not simply sit for weeks or months of a trial and then walk into the jury room with instant recall of all that had transpired. Jurors need to be engaged and to synthesize information as the trial proceeds. Although the Arizona judges, and other commentators, have not urged a return to the investigative role of the medieval juror or the law-determining role of the early American juror, they have agreed to procedural changes that would enable jurors to become active learners at an earlier point in the trial.

& Hum. Behav. 359 (2000) (studying the effect of permitting jurors to engage in preverdict deliberations in civil trials).

43. *See Waking Up Jurors, Shaking Up Courts*, Trial, July 1997, at 20 ("The 'passive juror' notion is an antiquated legal model that is neither educational nor democratic. It flies in the face of what we know about human nature to assume that jurors remain mentally passive, refrain from using preexisting frames of reference, consider and remember all the evidence, and suspend all judgment until they begin formal deliberations.") (quoting Arizona Superior Court Judge B. Michael Dann).

Chapter 4

Right to a Trial by Jury

In general, my approach is to examine the jury as an institution rather than describing the civil and criminal juries separately; however, the distinction between civil and criminal juries becomes important in a discussion of the constitutional right to a trial by jury. The reason is that two different constitutional amendments provide for jury trials in these two different contexts. The Sixth Amendment provides for a jury trial in criminal cases in federal court and the Seventh Amendment provides for a jury trial in certain types of civil cases in federal court. Accordingly, each of the constitutional bases for a right to a trial by jury will be considered in turn. It is important to keep in mind, however, that the defining features of the jury, whether the jury is hearing a criminal or civil case, are the same; therefore, the distinctions that are made in the constitutional discussion that follows will not be made elsewhere. In fact, Congress declined to distinguish between civil and criminal juries when providing that all juries meet certain threshold statutory requirements.[1]

1. *See* 28 U.S.C. §§ 1861 *et seq.*

Constitutional Right to a Trial by Jury

Sixth Amendment

The Sixth Amendment provides, in relevant part, that "[i]n all criminal prosecutions, the accused shall enjoy the right to a speedy and public trial, by an impartial jury of the State and district wherein the crime shall have been committed."[2] The Sixth Amendment applies to criminal defendants charged with serious federal crimes; it provides that they receive a jury trial in federal court. However, this right to a jury trial in a criminal proceeding in federal court has been interpreted by the U.S. Supreme Court as so fundamental—as so essential to a fair trial—that it applies to the States by virtue of the Due Process Clause of the Fourteenth Amendment. As the Court explained:

> Because we believe that trial by jury in criminal cases is fundamental to the American scheme of justice, we hold that the Fourteenth Amendment guarantees a right of jury trial in all criminal cases which—were they to be tried in a federal court—would come within the Sixth Amendment's guarantee.[3]

One reason that the Court viewed the Sixth Amendment's right to a jury trial as so fundamental to our system of justice was that it conceived of the jury as a buffer between the defendant and the government. In prosecuting a crime, the government wields extraordinary power. The jury is one

2. U.S. CONST. amend. VI.

3. Duncan v. Louisiana, 391 U.S. 145, 149 (1968).

vehicle for providing the criminal defendant with some protections, particularly against governmental actors who could potentially abuse their power. As Justice White explained in *Duncan v. Louisiana*, a jury in a criminal trial "prevent[s] oppression by the Government."[4] The jury stands between a defendant and an overzealous prosecutor who might bring unwarranted charges or between a defendant and a hardened judge who might no longer be attentive to protecting the defendant's rights.

Although the words of the Sixth Amendment provide that a criminal defendant has a right to a jury trial "[i]n *all* criminal prosecutions,"[5] the Supreme Court has interpreted that language to mean that a criminal defendant has a right to a jury trial in *all serious* criminal prosecutions. In spite of the literal language of the Sixth Amendment, the Court has long interpreted the right to a jury trial to apply only to serious or nonpetty crimes.[6] One question that the Court's interpretation of the Sixth Amendment raised is: How should courts decide between crimes that are serious and require a jury trial and those that are petty and do not require a jury trial? To answer this question, the Supreme Court looked at " 'the severity of the maximum authorized penalty.' "[7] In the Court's view, it was

4. *Id.* at 155.

5. U.S. Const. amend. VI (emphasis added).

6. *See* Blanton v. City of North Las Vegas, 489 U.S. 538, 541–42 (1989) (citing cases dating back to 1888).

7. *Id.* at 541 (quoting Baldwin v. New York, 399 U.S. 66, 68 (1970)).

reasonable to look at the penalty assigned by the legislature as an indication of the seriousness of the crime because judges should not substitute their judgment of a serious crime for that of legislators.

The conclusion the Court reached in *Blanton v. City of North Las Vegas* was that while the "penalty" need not be limited to the maximum prison term authorized by statute, the authorized prison term was a reasonable starting-point.[8] The Court has continued to abide by a test it formulated in an earlier case,[9] which is that whenever the maximum authorized prison time is *greater than six months,* the defendant is entitled to a jury trial.[10] The Court left open the possibility that an authorized prison term of *less* than six months, when coupled with other penalties, could constitute a "serious" offense for purposes of securing a jury trial. However, the Court noted that while this possibility exists, the *presumption* is that an authorized prison term of less than six months constitutes a petty offense for which there is no right to jury trial.

The Court illustrated how this presumption was to be applied in *United States v. Nachtigal.*[11] At issue in this case was whether defendant, charged with a driving-under-the-influence (DUI) violation

8. *Id.* at 542 ("In using the word 'penalty,' we do not refer solely to the maximum prison term authorized for a particular offense.").

9. *See* Baldwin v. New York, 399 U.S. 66, 69 & n.6 (1970) (plurality opinion).

10. *Blanton*, 489 U.S. at 542–43.

11. 507 U.S. 1 (1993) (*per curiam*).

that carried a maximum prison term of less than six months, was entitled to a jury trial. Given a prison term of under six months, the offense was presumptively petty, with no right to a jury trial attaching. The Court moved on to a consideration of the additional penalties—a fine and probation—that could be imposed. It concluded that they were insufficient to overcome the presumption, and therefore, defendant had no right to a jury trial in this case.

Although the Court has highlighted the importance of the right to a jury trial in criminal cases in federal court, particularly because of the protections it affords the criminal defendant, there is no comparable right to a trial before a judge. According to Rule 23(a) of the *Federal Rules of Criminal Procedure*, a defendant can waive his right to a jury trial in a case that requires a jury trial only if he has the consent of the government and the approval of the court.[12] When the petitioner in *Singer v. United States*,[13] who had been charged with thirty counts of mail fraud, sought a trial before a judge and the government refused to consent, petitioner argued that he had not only a right to a jury trial, but also a "correlative right to have his case decided by a judge alone if he considers such a trial to be to his advantage."[14] The Court rejected his argument because there had been no right at common law for a

---

12. Rule 23(a) provides: "Cases required to be tried by jury shall be so tried unless the defendant waives a jury trial in writing with the approval of the court and the consent of the government." FED. R. CRIM. P. 23(a).

13. 380 U.S. 24 (1965).

14. *Id.* at 25.

criminal defendant to choose between a trial before a jury and one before a judge. In addition, the colonists did not consider the right to a trial before a judge to be as fundamental as a right to a jury trial.

Although a defendant can waive his right to a jury trial, that waiver is not absolute. The Court found it reasonable to condition that waiver upon the consent of the government and the approval of the court, as encapsulated in Rule 23(a). If the government or the court does not consent, defendant is left with a trial by jury, which is "the very thing that the Constitution guarantees him."[15]

Seventh Amendment

The Seventh Amendment provides a right to a jury trial in federal court in certain civil cases. The challenge is in ascertaining which cases qualify for a jury trial. The language of the amendment offers limited guidance. It provides in relevant part: "In Suits at common law, where the value in controversy shall exceed twenty dollars, the right of trial by jury shall be preserved...."[16] Certainly, the twenty dollars no longer serves as a bar to a jury trial, though it might have in 1791 when the amendment was adopted. Rather, the Supreme Court, in trying to give effect to the amendment, has focused on the language of "preserv[ing]" the right to jury trial for "[s]uits at common law." The Court requires trial judges to ask two questions in deciding whether

15. *Id.* at 36.

16. U.S. Const. amend. VII.

there is a Seventh Amendment right to a jury trial: (1) What is the nature of the action (legal or equitable) being brought today and would that type of action have received a jury trial in 1791 when the Seventh Amendment was adopted? (2) What is the nature of the remedy being sought and would that type of remedy have been granted by a court of law or equity in 1791? If the remedy would have been granted by a court of law, then the remedy is one that is appropriate for a jury to decide; if it would have been granted by a court of equity, then it is one that would not be appropriate for a jury to decide.

Although this two-pronged historical test is one that is meant to embody the Seventh Amendment's commitment to "preserv[ing]" jury trials for "[s]uits at common law," it is not an easy test to apply. This is particularly so because many actions that are brought today did not exist in 1791. As a result, the trial judge must look for an analogous claim—a claim that existed in 1791 and that resembles today's claim—to see if the earlier claim received a jury trial. However, the fit between today's claim and the earlier, analogous claim is often inexact and there can be competing analogous claims. In addition, it is not always clear how the two prongs of the historical test work together. The Court has said that the second prong carries more weight than the first, but how much more? And how is that translated into practice?

As an illustration of the difficulties, consider *Local 391 v. Terry*.[17] In that case, several employees of

McLean Trucking Company were laid off, and then reinstated but stripped of their seniority rights. The employees initiated grievance procedures and eventually filed a lawsuit in federal district court. They alleged that the company had breached the collective-bargaining agreement in violation of § 301 of the Labor Management Relations Act[18] and that the union had violated its duty of fair representation. They sought reinstatement and compensatory damages for lost benefits and wages. After the company went bankrupt, the suit continued solely against the union. The former employees sought a jury trial and the union moved to strike the demand on the ground that there is no right to a jury trial in a breach of duty of fair representation suit.

Although the judgment of the Supreme Court was that the former employees *did* have a right to a jury trial in their breach of duty of fair representation suit, the Justices disagreed as to why this was so. Justice Marshall, who announced the judgment of the Court, looked first at the action for breach of a union's duty of fair representation, and because it did not exist in 1791 in England, he searched for an appropriate analogue. He concluded that a breach of duty of fair representation action resembled most closely an action by a trust beneficiary against a trustee for breach of a fiduciary duty. Such a trust action would have been equitable in nature, which would mean no jury trial. However, he viewed the

17.   494 U.S. 558 (1990).

18.   29 U.S.C. § 185.

breach of the collective-bargaining agreement, which also must be proven in any breach of duty of fair representation action, as comparable to a breach of contract claim. Such a claim would be legal in nature, meaning that it would receive a jury trial. Thus, the first prong of the test resulted in a situation of "equipoise":[19] one claim (breach of duty of fair representation) was equitable and would not have been heard by a jury and one claim (breach of the collective-bargaining agreement) was legal and would have been heard by a jury. Justice Marshall concluded, however, that the tie was broken by the second (and as the Court had said in the past, more important) prong of the test. The employees sought damages, and these were legal rather than equitable in nature; therefore, a right to a jury trial attached.

Five other Justices agreed with the result that Justice Marshall reached, but two of them disagreed as to the reasoning. Justice Brennan thought the first prong of the test too difficult to apply; he wrote separately urging the Court to abandon the first prong of the test. He reasoned that Justices and trial judges were not historians and "there remain[ed] little purpose to [their] rattling through dusty attics of ancient writs."[20] He would rely wholly upon the second prong of the test—the nature of the remedy—which is the prong the Court had said in earlier cases should be given greater weight.[21]

19.   494 U.S. at 570.

20.   *Id.* at 576.

21.   *Id.* at 575 ("For the past decade and a half, this Court has explained that the two parts of the historical test are not

Justice Stevens reached the same result as Justices Brennan and Marshall, but he did so by comparing the breach of duty of fair representation action to the common-law action against an attorney for malpractice. He believed that this analogue, which was historically an action at law, bore a closer resemblance to a breach of duty of fair representation than did an action against a trustee. It was unrealistic, he wrote, to expect to find an exact analogue. The best a court could do was to find "a useful analogy"[22] and to take care not to curtail the right to a jury trial, particularly if the action was one that called for "the common sense understanding of the jury,"[23] as did a breach of duty of fair representation claim or a malpractice claim.

Justice Kennedy, joined in his dissent by Justices O'Connor and Scalia, agreed with Justice Marshall that the better analogue was the trust action rather than a legal malpractice action. However, he parted company with Justice Marshall in that he would not consider the breach of the collective-bargaining agreement separately. Thus, because the duty of fair representation claim resembled the trust action and the trust action was equitable in nature, the claim did not require a jury trial. He also reasoned that the remedy of damages was not always legal in nature and that courts of equity could and did award the kind of damages sought by the former

equal in weight, that the nature of the remedy is more important than the nature of the right.").

22. *Id.* at 583.

23. *Id.*

employees. Thus, the request for damages did not entitle the former employees to a jury under the Seventh Amendment. Justice Kennedy also rejected Justice Brennan's approach that they abandon the first prong of the test. He felt that to do so would require rewriting the Constitution.[24]

Although the historical test is difficult to apply, as the above case illustrates, the difficulties are limited to federal courts. The Supreme Court has never held that the Seventh Amendment is applicable to the States through the Fourteenth Amendment,[25] as it has with the Sixth Amendment.[26] As a result, the two-pronged historical test, "requiring

24. Justice Brennan, however, had not recommended wholesale abandonment of an historical approach. He would still maintain the second prong of the test, which required judges to look to the remedy and whether it would have been granted by a court of equity or law. Thus, he would have retained an historical component, albeit limited to the second prong of the test. Although Justice Kennedy rejected Justice Brennan's approach as too much of a deviation from what the Constitution requires, in fact, the test devised by the Court is not written in the Constitution, but was formulated by the Justices in their attempt to give meaning to the Seventh Amendment.

25. *See* Gasperini v. Center for Humanities, 518 U.S. 415, 418 (1996) ("Seventh Amendment ... governs proceedings in federal court, but not in state court."); Curtis v. Loether, 415 U.S. 189, 192 n.6 (1974) (noting that the Supreme Court "has not held that the right to jury trial in civil cases is an element of due process applicable to state courts through the Fourteenth Amendment"); *see also* GTFM v. TKN Sales, 257 F.3d 235 (2d Cir. 2001) ("The Seventh Amendment has not, however, been applied to the States through the Fourteenth Amendment and hence does not require that jury trials be held in proceedings in State tribunals.").

26. *See supra* text accompanying notes 2–4.

extensive and possibly abstruse historical inqui-ry,"[27] is a matter with which federal, but not state, court judges must contend.

Statutory Right to a Trial by Jury

Another way in which a party to a civil suit may have a right to a jury trial in federal court is if Congress, in creating a new statutory cause of action, also provides that a right to a jury trial will attach.

In *Feltner v. Columbia Pictures Television*,[28] which focused on § 504(c) of the Copyright Act, the Supreme Court considered whether the statute pro-vided a right to a jury trial. Only after finding that the statute was "silent on the point,"[29] did the Court move to a consideration of the Seventh Amendment. The Court focused first on the statute because if the statute resolved the question, then the Court would have been able to avoid reaching a constitutional question. Although § 504(c) did not reveal " 'any congressional intent to grant the right to a jury trial,' "[30] the Court's approach did make clear that it is within Congress's power to do so.

As *Feltner v. Columbia Pictures Television* illus-trated, Congress also could enact a statute creating a new cause of action and explicitly not provide for a jury trial; in that case, if a jury trial is sought, the

27. Ross v. Bernhard, 396 U.S. 531, 538 n.10 (1970).

28. 523 U.S. 340 (1998).

29. *Id.* at 342.

30. *Id.* at 345 (quoting Tull v. United States, 481 U.S. 412, 417 n.3 (1987)).

trial judge must apply the two-pronged historical test of the Seventh Amendment to determine whether the Seventh Amendment provides a jury trial. Even though the new cause of action would clearly not have existed in 1791, the Seventh Amendment's right to a jury trial is not limited to actions that existed then. The Supreme Court made this point in *Curtis v. Loether*:

> [W]e have considered the applicability of the constitutional right to jury trial in actions enforcing statutory rights 'as a matter too obvious to be doubted.' . . . Although the Court has apparently never discussed the issue at any length, we have often found the Seventh Amendment applicable to causes of action based on statutes.[31]

Implementation of the Right to Trial by Jury

Although the Sixth and Seventh Amendments of the U.S. Constitution, as interpreted by the U.S. Supreme Court, provide the scope of a right to jury trial, Congress provided uniform procedures for implementing the right to a jury trial in federal court that apply in both civil and criminal cases.

Relevant Statutes

In 28 U.S.C. §§ 1861 *et seq.*, Congress provided basic threshold requirements for summoning and selecting jurors. Congress adopted the more protective standards of the Sixth Amendment, as interpreted by the Supreme Court, and has made these requirements applicable to *all* jury trials in federal court. In all cases, for example, jurors must be

31.   415 U.S. 189, 193 (1974) (citation omitted).

drawn from "a fair cross section of the community."[32] Although this language is not found explicitly in the Sixth Amendment, the Supreme Court has interpreted the Sixth Amendment's requirement of an "impartial jury" to mean one in which jurors are drawn from "a fair cross section" of the community.[33] To give further effect to this requirement, Congress has explicitly provided that "[n]o citizen shall be excluded from service ... on account of race, color, religion, sex, national origin, or economic status."[34] Congress also has tried to give more precise meaning to "a fair cross section of the community" by requiring districts to draw up plans for random jury selection,[35] by carefully delineating the responsibilities of the jury commissioner or clerk in jury selection,[36] and by expanding the lists from which prospective jurors' names are drawn.[37]

Congress also created uniform qualifications for all jurors in federal courts, whether they are called to serve in a civil or criminal case or on a grand or petit jury.[38] Under 28 U.S.C. § 1865, any citizen is qualified to serve unless he or she: is not a citizen at least eighteen years old who has lived in the

32. 28 U.S.C. § 1861.

33. Taylor v. Louisiana, 419 U.S. 522 (1975).

34. 28 U.S.C. § 1862.

35. 28 U.S.C. § 1863.

36. 28 U.S.C. § 1863(b)(1) & (3).

37. 28 U.S.C. § 1863(b)(2) ("The plan shall prescribe some other source or sources of names in addition to voter lists where necessary to foster the policy and protect the rights secured by sections 1861 and 1862 of this title.").

38. 28 U.S.C. § 1865.

judicial district for at least one year; is unable to read, write, understand or speak English; is unable to serve because of a mental or physical incapacity; or has a charge pending for a crime or has been convicted of a crime punishable by more than one year of imprisonment.[39]

Finally, Congress has provided by statute uniform protections for jurors. For example, jurors receive the same pay, whether they serve in a civil or criminal trial.[40] They also receive protection against dismissal from their jobs as a result of their jury service[41] and compensation for a disability incurred during jury service.[42] In all of these areas, Congress extended the same protections to jurors whether they serve in a criminal or civil trial.

Relevant Rules

As a practical matter, the federal rules distinguish between a right to a jury trial in a civil or a criminal case in one important respect. In a criminal case to be tried by a jury, *Federal Rule of Criminal Procedure* 23(a) provides that the defendant has a right to a jury trial unless he waives it in writing with the consent of the government and the approval of the court.[43] In contrast, in any civil matter in which there is a right to a jury trial, either party must make a demand for a jury trial.[44]

39. 28 U.S.C. § 1865(b).

40. 28 U.S.C. § 1871.

41. 28 U.S.C. § 1875.

42. 28 U.S.C. § 1877.

43. Fed. R. Crim. P. 23(a).

44. Fed. R. Civ. P. 38(b).

A party does this by serving the demand upon the other parties as well as by filing it with the court, as required by Rule 5(d).[45] Failure to serve and file a demand will result in waiver of a party's right to a jury trial.[46] Thus, the default position in each is different: in a serious criminal matter there is a jury trial unless it is waived with consent; in a civil matter there is a bench trial unless a demand for a jury trial is made, and failure to take this affirmative step results in waiver of the right to a jury trial. However, failure to demand a jury trial is not always fatal: if a party neglects to make a demand, the court still retains the discretion to order a jury trial on any or all issues once a motion is made.[47]

45. *Id.*
46. FED. R. CIV. P. 38(d).
47. FED. R. CIV. P. 39(b).

Chapter 5

Jury Selection

One way to understand jury selection is to see that it occurs in stages. The first stage is the summoning of the *venire* or the panel of prospective jurors from which the petit jury is selected. The second stage is the *voir dire* or the questioning of prospective jurors so that the parties can learn about their backgrounds and attitudes. The third stage is the exercise of *for cause challenges*, to remove those prospective jurors who cannot be impartial or who do not satisfy the appearance of impartiality, and the exercise of *peremptory challenges*, to allow the parties to remove a limited number of prospective jurors whom they would rather not have on their jury. The voir dire and the exercise of challenges are two distinct phases but they can overlap, particularly with the exercise of for cause challenges, which are usually made during the course of the voir dire. The jurors who are selected for the petit jury are then asked to stand and to take an oath according to which they swear to hear the evidence without prejudice and to decide the case fairly. At this juncture, the jury has been empanelled and the trial can commence.

Venire

*A Key Legal Issue: The Fair Cross-
Section Requirement*

The main constitutional issue raised by the summoning of a venire is whether those summoned
represent a "fair cross section" of the community.
Although the Supreme Court has held that the
Sixth Amendment's requirement of an "impartial
jury" can be satisfied only if jurors in a criminal
case are drawn from a fair cross-section of the
community, Congress has extended this requirement to civil cases as well. Thus, for all venires,
whether for civil or criminal cases, the prospective
jurors must be drawn from a fair cross-section of
the community.

The Supreme Court has given some guidance,
albeit fairly general, as to what constitutes a fair
cross-section. At the very least, a fair cross-section
means that no group has been systematically excluded from the venire. In a case that was decided
under a court's supervisory powers, the Supreme
Court considered why it was important for the jury
system that no group be systematically excluded
from the venire. In *Thiel v. Southern Pacific Co.*,[1]
daily wage earners were systematically excluded
from a venire in a case in which the petitioner
claimed that the railroad had acted negligently in
allowing him to travel when " 'out of his normal
mind' " and to jump out of the window of the
moving train.[2] Petitioner contended that the exclu-

1. 328 U.S. 217 (1946).
2. *Id.* at 219.

sion of daily wage earners meant that the venire
would be filled with people who saw the case from
the railroad's, rather than from a working-man's,
point of view.

The Jury Commissioner had excluded daily wage
earners, not through malevolent design, but because he believed that those who earned their wages
on a day-to-day basis would suffer economic hardship if they had to forgo those wages in order to
perform jury service. The Jury Commissioner assumed that daily wage earners would plead economic hardship, and thus, he did not even summon
them to serve. The Supreme Court concluded, however, that the exclusion of daily wage earners "however well-intentioned and however justified by prior
actions of trial judges, must be counted among
those tendencies which undermine and weaken the
institution of the jury."[3] The jury system would be
weakened if only the economically and socially privileged served as jurors. The Court held that the
systematic exclusion of daily wage earners could not
be justified and that petitioner was entitled to "a
new trial by a jury drawn from a panel properly and
fairly chosen."[4]

To challenge the venire as improperly drawn, one
need not be a member of the group that has been
excluded. For example, in *Peters v. Kiff*,[5] the defendant, a white man, sought to challenge the venire
from which his jury had been drawn. The defendant

3. *Id.* at 224.

4. *Id.* at 225.

5. 407 U.S. 493 (1972).

claimed that African-American men[6] had been systematically excluded from the venires from which the grand jury that indicted him and the petit jury that convicted him of burglary had been drawn.

The Supreme Court concluded that if the allegations were true, such selection practices violated the Constitution regardless of the circumstances of the person making the claim.[7] Several Justices, in considering the harm to the defendant, believed that a venire from which African-American men had been excluded would violate a defendant's right to due process[8] in that the "exclusion deprives the jury of a perspective on human events that may have unsuspected importance in any case that may be presented."[9] Although this due process theory garnered the support of only three Justices (Justices Marshall, Douglas, and Stewart), six Justices joined the judgment of the Court to hold that the arbitrary exclusion of African-American men from the venire violated the Constitution and that the challenge

6. In the early 1970s, women of any race were still not required to be summoned for the venire in order to satisfy the fair cross-section requirement. As late as 1961, the Court had upheld Florida's practice of requiring only women to register affirmatively for jury duty even though it meant that women would be significantly underrepresented on the venire. Hoyt v. Florida, 368 U.S. 57 (1961); *see infra* text accompanying notes 10–18.

7. 407 U.S. at 498.

8. A Sixth Amendment claim was unavailable to the defendant because his case was decided prior to *Duncan v. Louisiana*, 391 U.S. 145 (1968), which made the Sixth Amendment applicable to the states through the Fourteenth Amendment.

9. 407 U.S. at 503–04.

could be raised by a defendant regardless of his race.

The acceptability of excluding certain groups from the venire without violating the fair cross-section requirement has changed over time. Until *Taylor v. Louisiana*,[10] women could be systematically excluded from the venire without violating the Constitution. In the past, this exclusion has taken different forms. One form was the requirement that women, but not men, affirmatively register to be considered for jury service. This exclusion, like the blanket exclusion of daily wage earners by the Jury Commissioner in *Thiel v. Southern Pacific*, discussed *supra*, was motivated not necessarily by animus toward women, but by a view that women were needed to take care of the home and children, and therefore, would be unable to serve as jurors. As a result of affirmative registration, women were summoned in disproportionately small numbers compared to their numbers in the community. In 1961, the Court upheld this practice in *Hoyt v. Florida*,[11] thus denying Ms. Hoyt's claim that a venire that excluded women violated her right to Due Process under the Fourteenth Amendment.

Almost fifteen years later, in the 1975 case of *Taylor v. Louisiana*,[12] the Supreme Court reversed its decision in *Hoyt* and held that the practice of affirmative registration violated a defendant's Sixth Amendment right to a venire drawn from a fair

10.　419 U.S. 522 (1975).

11.　368 U.S. 57 (1961).

12.　419 U.S. 522 (1975).

cross-section of the community. Defendant Billy Taylor challenged the venire from which his petit jury was drawn because it contained no women. Both defendant and the State stipulated that the discrepancy between the number of women eligible for jury duty in that district and those actually included in the venire was attributable to the practice of requiring women to register for jury service. The Court reasoned that any practice that excluded 53% of the citizenry from jury duty, as did Louisiana's practice of affirmative registration for women, violated the fair cross-section requirement.

Although the Court believed that this practice might once have been justified by women's traditional role in the family, that traditional role no longer pertained, and even if it did in some women's cases, those cases could be decided individually rather than assuming that most women could not serve. The Court acknowledged the change in norms:

> If at one time it could be held that Sixth Amendment juries must be drawn from a fair cross section of the community but that this requirement permitted the almost total exclusion of women, this is not the case today. Communities differ at different times and places. What is a fair cross section at one time or place is not necessarily a fair cross section at another time or a different place.[13]

13. *Id.* at 537.

The Court's decision was limited to the venire and did not impose any requirements on the representativeness of the petit jury. The Court's decision also applied to "distinctive groups in the community," such as women, and left it to the discretion of the states to develop procedures so that juries were drawn from venires that were "reasonably representative."[14]

The Court developed the issue further in *Duren v. Missouri*,[15] in which it had to decide how representative a venire must be in order to satisfy the fair cross-section requirement of the Sixth Amendment. In *Duren*, the defendant challenged a venire in which only 14.5% of its members were women, in a community in which 54% of those eligible to serve as jurors were women. The Court articulated a prima facie test that a defendant challenging the representativeness of a venire must satisfy. Such a defendant must show that: (1) the group alleged to be excluded is a "distinctive" group in the community; (2) the representation of this group on venires is not "fair and reasonable" in relation to their numbers in the community; and (3) the underrepresentation is due to systematic exclusion of the group in the jury selection process.[16]

The Court in *Duren* accepted defendant's statistics and agreed that he had established a prima facie case that his venire violated the fair cross-section requirement of the Sixth Amendment.

14. *Id.* at 538.
15. 439 U.S. 357 (1979).
16. *Id.* at 364.

Women were a "distinctive" group, as *Taylor* had established, and Duren had shown that they made up over half the population of his county, but constituted only 14.5% of the venire from which his jury was drawn. The Court "disagree[d] with the conclusion of the court below that jury venires containing approximately 15% women are 'reasonably representative' of this community."[17] Finally, Duren was able to show that women's exclusion was "systematic" in that there was a large discrepancy between their numbers on the venire and their numbers in the community and that this discrepancy had occurred in every weekly venire for a period of almost a year. In addition, Duren showed that this occurred because of Missouri's system of granting automatic exemptions to all women; their numbers dropped when they were summoned and permitted to claim an automatic exemption, as well as later on in the selection process, when they did not respond and were presumed to have exercised their automatic exemption.

The inquiry does not end once the defendant satisfies the prima facie test; rather, the State then bears the burden of showing a significant state interest in its practice. In *Duren*, Missouri failed to offer any "substantial justification" for the automatic exemption, other than "safeguarding the important role played by women in home and family life."[18] Although the Court did not rule out the possibility that a state could tailor an exemption for

17. *Id.* at 365–66.
18. *Id.* at 369.

those with family responsibilities, Missouri had not done so. The Court urged states to tread carefully when exempting broad categories of citizens from jury service; otherwise, they would run afoul of the fair cross-section requirement, as Missouri had done in *Duren*.

Policy Issues

Multiple Source Lists. Although the Supreme Court and Congress have been clear that venires must be drawn from a "fair cross section" of the community, it has not always been easy for courts and court administrators to figure out how to draw such venires.

One policy question that has arisen in the context of venires has been: from which source lists should venires be drawn? Traditionally, prospective jurors have been summoned from voter registration lists. One justification for using a voter registration list is that jury service, like voting, is a badge of citizenship. A voter registration list is more likely than other lists to contain names of those who would also qualify as jurors. In addition, a voter registration list, which contains the names of those who not only qualify as voters but also have taken the affirmative step of registering to vote, might be a more reliable list. The assumption is that registered voters are more likely to respond positively to a jury summons; they have already demonstrated their commitment to performing the civic duty of regis-tering to vote, so perhaps they also will perform their other civic duty of responding to their jury summons.

For a long time, the preference for drawing prospective jurors from only voter registration lists prevailed. In the 1970s, however, a number of academics recommended that voter registration lists be supplemented by other lists, such as taxpayer rolls, drivers' licenses, unemployment and welfare rolls, and telephone and utility lists.[19] They believed that voter registration lists were underrepresentative of certain groups, such as racial minorities, people under forty, those with lower incomes and less education, blue-collar workers, and the unemployed.[20] The hope was that by supplementing traditional voter registration lists with some of these other lists, prospective jurors would be drawn from a broader swath of the community.

Although there is still debate today about precisely which lists should supplement voter registration lists,[21] there is greater agreement that supplemental

19. *See, e.g.*, David Kairys et al., *Jury Representativeness: A Mandate for Multiple Source Lists*, 65 CAL. L. REV. 776 (1977).

20. *See id.* at 826.

21. For example, in one case, *United States v. Hanson*, 618 F.2d 1261 (8th Cir. 1980), defendants argued that the venire was improperly drawn because the court had failed to use a tribal enrollment list as a supplement to the voter registration list. *Id.* at 1267. Minnesota's plan required it to select jurors from voter registration lists. Defendants argued that the voter registration list did not include those who had voted in Red Lake Tribal elections. The Eighth Circuit was not persuaded; it attributed any shortcomings of the voter registration list to those Red Lake residents who failed to register to vote. *Id.*

lists should be used. According to one study, "[a]s of August 1996, 12 states use only voter registration lists, six states use only lists of licensed drivers, two states use state-unique lists, and 25 use a combined voters and drivers list. Five states add some additional lists to the voters and drivers lists."[22] Even today, jurisdictions that use only a voter registration list are likely to have venires in which older, upper-income, well-educated, and nonminority citizens are overrepresented.[23]

Stratified Juror Selection. One way to make venires more representative is to use multiple source lists; another, more experimental, method is to use "stratified juror selection."[24] The latter method entails "manipulating the number of citizens in each of several multiple smaller lists who are summoned, qualified, or sent questionnaires" so as to provide "that each of several populations is sampled proportionally."[25] This might mean that some typically underrepresented populations on the venire are sent more questionnaires to increase their numbers and that other typically overrepresented populations are sent fewer questionnaires to reduce their numbers on the venire. However, even with this method, proportional representation of different racial and ethnic groups is not guaranteed. For example, residents still may not receive or return the questionnaires, qualify for jury service,

22. JURY TRIAL INNOVATIONS 36 (G. Thomas Munsterman et al. eds., 1997)

23. *Id.* at 35.

24. Nancy J. King & G. Thomas Munsterman, *Stratified Juror Selection: Cross-Section by Design*, 79 JUDICATURE 273 (1996).

25. *Id.* at 274..

or be summoned in proportion to their numbers in the community. One variation adopted by some jurisdictions, such as New York, is to send out questionnaires and summonses based on past response rates by zip code. In those zip codes in which past response rates have been weak, additional questionnaires are mailed.

Although the aim of these stratified methods—to have the venire mirror residential demographics—is not new, what is new is the use of small geographic areas, such as zip codes rather than counties, as well as the court's intervention at the questionnaire and summonses stages, rather than at the earlier stage of compiling names for the master wheel.

District courts have been innovative in their approaches to stratified jury selection, but appellate courts have not always approved of these efforts. For example, in the Eastern District of Michigan, the court randomly struck a certain number of " 'white and other' " qualified prospective jurors to preserve a venire with racial demographics that mirrored that of the community.[26] However, in *United States v. Ovalle*,[27] the Sixth Circuit struck down this "subtraction method" of stratified jury

26. *Id.* at 275.

27. 136 F.3d 1092 (6th Cir. 1998).

selection, holding that it violated the Jury Selection and Service Act[28] (JSSA) and the equal protection component of the Fifth Amendment. The Sixth Circuit held that the subtraction method violated 28 U.S.C. § 1862 of the JSSA, which provides that "no citizen shall be excluded from service as a grand or petit juror ... on account of race, color, religion, sex, national origin, or economic status."[29] A practice that removed the names of Hispanics and other individuals "for the sole reason that they were not African-Americans"[30] violated the ban against racial exclusion contained in § 1862.

The Sixth Circuit also held that the practice violated the equal protection component of the Fifth Amendment because even though the government had a compelling interest for its practice, the government had not tailored the practice as narrowly as it could have to meet that interest.[31] The Sixth Circuit noted that the practice did not assure adequate representation on the jury wheel for Hispanics or any other group except for African-Americans. In the Sixth Circuit's view, there were other methods, such as multiple source lists, to expand

28. 28 U.S.C. §§ 1861 *et seq.*

29. 28 U.S.C. § 1862.

30. *Ovalle*, 136 F.3d at 1100.

31. *See id.* at 1106.

the jury pool, and the method chosen by the Eastern District of Michigan violated the Constitution because it removed people from the jury wheel "solely on the basis of race."[32]

Improving Responses to Jury Summonses. Yet another method for making venires more representative is to improve prospective jurors' response rates to jury summonses. If response rates increase, particularly among groups that are not traditionally well-represented on venires, such as those who are members of a minority group, poor, or under age forty, then venires will move closer toward truly representing a fair cross-section of the community.

Jurisdictions have experimented with both carrot-and-stick approaches to improving prospective jurors' response rates. The stick approach typically consists of threatening those who ignore their summons with a fine and/or jail time. In California, failure to appear for jury duty is an act of contempt punishable by a fine of up to $1000 and five days in jail.[33] Although most counties in California do not actually impose such penalties, a few, such as Stanislaus County, have developed reputations for toughness. In Stanislaus County, a "failure to appear" postcard follows an ignored jury summons, and if that does not elicit a response within ten days, then a uniformed marshal with an order to show cause can appear at the door.[34] In Los Angeles

32. *Id.*

33. *See* Greg Moran, *When Jury Duty Calls: Counties Wrestle with High Evasion Rates*, CAL. LAW., May 2001, at 22.

34. *Id.*

County, some prospective jurors who have ignored their summons have been fined as much as $1000 in part to remind them that jury duty is not voluntary and in part to serve as an example to others who have failed to respond.

The carrot approach entails both teaching citizens and students about jury service and improving the jury experience so that it is less off-putting for prospective jurors. Some jurisdictions have embarked upon educational outreach, running ad campaigns with slogans such as Duluth, Minnesota's "It Isn't Fair, If You're Not There," or Pittsburgh, Pennsylvania's "Jury Service: Your Role in the Justice System."[35] The former included mailers for distribution in low-income and minority areas in Duluth to reach members of these communities.

In other areas, civic groups have focused on outreach to the schools. By teaching students about jury service when they are young, the hope is that they will respond positively to their jury summons when they are of age to serve. One group in Washington, D.C., the Council for Court Excellence, organized a "You Decide" campaign that includes an educational package and a teacher's guide about the jury; it is now used by school systems in about twenty states.[36]

Efforts to make jury service more pleasant have ranged from the substantive to the superficial. One substantive change has been the move by many

35. JURY TRIAL INNOVATIONS, *supra* note 22, at 26–27.
36. *Id.* at 27.

jurisdictions[37] to "one day/one trial," in which prospective jurors must report for jury duty and if they
are not selected for a jury on that first day, then
they have fulfilled their obligation to serve until the
next time they are called. If they are selected for a
trial on that day, then they serve for that trial only.
The main advantage to this practice is that it elimi-
nates the waiting time (that had typically spanned a
ten-day period) during which prospective jurors had
to report to the courthouse to see if they would be
selected for a jury. Another significant change for
jurors has been the increase in juror pay in a
number of jurisdictions, including New Jersey
which has increased juror pay from \$5 to \$40 per
day.

There have been other small changes that have
nonetheless improved the quality of life for jurors.
Examples of these include allowing prospective jurors to call in by telephone to see if their attendance
is required rather than making them report to the
courthouse for this purpose, equipping jury facilities
with telephones and quiet work areas so that jurors
can do their own work during court recesses and
times that do not require their attendance in court,
and improving courthouse facilities, such as providing working bathrooms in state courthouses in New
York.

Although all of these efforts are steps in the right
direction, yet another way to improve response

---

37. The practice is used statewide in Massachusetts, Connecticut, Florida, and Colorado, and by most courts in New York,
Arizona, North Carolina, and Texas. *Id.* at 29. As of 1997,
approximately 40% of all U.S. citizens lived in jurisdictions that
used one-day/one-trial systems. *Id.*

rates to jury summonses is to ask jury-eligible citizens why they responded or failed to respond to jury summonses. Several academic studies have revealed different reasons why prospective jurors do not always respond positively to summonses. In one study, the researchers found that prospective jurors who had been permitted to postpone their jury service and reschedule it for a more convenient time were enthusiastic about their jury service, even more so than those who actually reported for jury duty when called; those who had sought and had been denied an excuse were the most disgruntled.[38] The researchers hypothesized that when jurors could exercise some control over their jury service, they had a more positive feeling toward it.[39]

Another study identified several reasons why jury-eligible citizens did not respond to jury summonses.[40] One common reason was that summonses had been sent to old addresses, and therefore, were never received. Other reasons included prospective jurors' belief that they would not be penalized for their failure to respond, that they would not be compensated by their employers for jury service, that they would not be competent to serve (among those with less money and education), or that they would spend much time waiting and would ulti-

38. Susan Carol Losh et al., *"Reluctant Jurors": What Summons Responses Reveal about Jury Duty Attitudes*, 83 JUDICATURE 304, 310 (2000).

39. *Id.*

40. ROBERT G. BOATRIGHT, IMPROVING CITIZEN RESPONSE TO JURY SUMMONSES: A REPORT WITH RECOMMENDATIONS ix-x (American Judicature Society, 1998).

mately not be permitted to serve (among those with more money and education). This study also recommended different reforms to address the different reasons that prospective jurors failed to respond to their jury summons. For example, the study suggested court enforcement of summonses to alter the view that there was no penalty for failure to respond; it recommended updated mailing lists to correct the problem of summonses not being sent to current addresses.[41]

Voir Dire

The voir dire, or questioning of prospective jurors, is supposed to reveal which prospective jurors can be impartial and can serve on the petit jury and which cannot and should be removed either through the exercise of for cause or peremptory challenges.

A Key Legal Issue: Which Questions Must Be Asked?

One key constitutional issue raised by the voir dire is which questions does a party have a right to ask prospective jurors (or have the judge ask) under the Sixth and Fourteenth Amendments? Typically, this issue arises in the criminal context, although it is not limited to this setting. Criminal defendants have argued that they have a right to ask those questions that will help them to uncover prospective jurors' biases so that the jury that ultimately tries them is an "impartial jury" as guaranteed by the Sixth Amendment. Criminal defendants also have argued that their right to ask certain ques-

41. *Id.* at xii-xiii.

tions is protected by the Due Process Clause of the Fourteenth Amendment, which guarantees a fair trial and an impartial decisionmaker.

Although the Sixth and Fourteenth Amendments afford these general protections, it has not always been clear which questions are constitutionally required and which ones are simply advisable to ask. In *Ham v. South Carolina*,[42] petitioner was a young, bearded African-American man who was active in the civil rights movement in the South during the late 1960s. He was charged with possession of marijuana, a violation of state law. During the voir dire, he requested that the trial judge, who conducted the voir dire, ask four questions of prospective jurors. The first two questions pertained to possible racial prejudice, the third raised the issue of prejudice against bearded men, and the fourth related to pretrial publicity about the perceived drug problem in the country at that time. The trial judge asked a general question about racial prejudice, as required by South Carolina statute, but otherwise declined to ask any of petitioner's questions during the voir dire. Petitioner was tried, convicted, and sentenced to eighteen months in prison.

The U.S. Supreme Court, in an opinion by then Justice Rehnquist, held that the trial judge violated petitioner's right to due process by not inquiring more specifically about racial prejudice, but that the trial judge was not obligated by the Fourteenth Amendment to ask prospective jurors about any possible prejudice they might have toward bearded

42.   409 U.S. 524 (1973).

men.[43] The opinion did not offer much reasoning that would assist trial judges in drawing the line between those questions that are required by due process and those that are not. As to the questions pertaining to racial prejudice, the Court simply concluded: "[T]he Fourteenth Amendment requires that under the facts shown by this record the petitioner be permitted to have the jurors interrogated on the issue of racial bias."[44] As to the question pertaining to bias toward beards, the Court concluded: "The trial judge's refusal to inquire as to particular bias against beards, after his inquiries as to bias in general, does not reach the level of a constitutional violation."[45]

Justices Douglas and Marshall concurred in part and dissented in part, though each wrote separately to explain his reasoning. Both agreed that the trial judge was constitutionally required to ask about racial prejudice; both agreed with each other that the trial judge was required to ask about bias toward beards, but each offered a different rationale. For Justice Douglas, hair was a means by which people made important statements about themselves and their views; it was also a symbol that others might misinterpret.[46] Jurors might draw any number of conclusions, however unfounded, about men who sport beards, including that they engage in drug use or advocate unconventional lifestyles.

43. *Id.* at 527–28.

44. *Id.* at 527.

45. *Id.* at 528.

46. *Id.* at 529–30.

At the very least, the judge should have asked prospective jurors about any prejudices they harbored toward bearded men. For Justice Marshall, prejudice based on beards, like prejudice based on race, interfered with the impartial decisionmaker guaranteed to petitioner. Justice Marshall pointed out that in this case, it would have added little time for the trial judge to inquire about prejudice toward bearded men and that the absolute ban on this question did not strike the proper balance between fairness and efficiency.[47]

The law, as it stands, is that voir dire questions pertaining to racial prejudice are constitutionally protected, whereas voir dire questions pertaining to prejudice toward those with beards are not. Although the Court was careful to leave the trial judge great discretion in how he or she formulated the questions and in the number of questions posed, at the very least, the question about racial prejudice is required in a situation, like petitioner's, where there is the potential for such prejudice. To the extent the Court provided any reasons for its conclusion, it explained that the Fourteenth Amendment was enacted as one of the protections against racial discrimination. Although, as Justice Marshall pointed out, prejudice of any sort would interfere with a defendant's right to a fair trial and an impartial jury, the Court, albeit with sparse reasoning, tried to strike a balance: the voir dire questions should be sufficiently probing to elicit prejudice that might preclude a fair trial by an impartial jury, but

47. *Id.* at 533–34.

should not be so intrusive as to interfere with matters best left to the discretion of the trial judge.

A more recent case raised the issue of constitutionally required voir dire questions when prospective jurors have been exposed to extensive pretrial publicity. In *Mu'Min v. Virginia*,[48] Dawud Majid Mu'Min, a prisoner who had been out on a work detail, was charged with the murder and robbery of Gladys Nopwasky, a shop owner. There had been extensive newspaper coverage of the case prior to Mu'Min's trial, including his confession, the details of the crime, and debate about the feasibility of work-release programs for prisoners. Mu'Min submitted sixty-four questions for the judge to ask during voir dire and filed a motion for individual voir dire. The trial judge denied the motion and ruled that the prospective jurors would be questioned as a group. However, the prospective jurors would be further questioned in panels of four about the pretrial publicity to which they had been exposed. The judge agreed to ask twenty-four of the sixty-four proposed questions, but declined to ask the questions pertaining to the contents of what prospective jurors had read or heard about the case in the media.

Upon questioning the first group of twenty-six prospective jurors, the trial judge learned that sixteen had heard about the case from media accounts. The judge asked them whether they could still decide the case with an open mind. One juror said that he could not and was removed. In subsequent

48. 500 U.S. 415 (1991).

panels of four, whenever a prospective juror indicated that he had read about the case, he was asked whether he could be impartial. All who were eventually seated, including those who had read about the case beforehand, said that they could hear the case with an open mind. One prospective juror who had hesitated about whether she could proceed with an open mind had been removed by the trial judge *sua sponte*. Another was dismissed for cause because her responses had not seemed forthcoming. A jury of fourteen, including two alternates, was eventually seated. Eight of the twelve jurors who heard petitioner's case had been exposed to news coverage of it beforehand.

Mu'Min argued that the Fourteenth Amendment required the trial judge to inquire about the contents of the news coverage to which prospective jurors had been exposed; however, the U.S. Supreme Court rejected this argument. In an opinion written by Chief Justice Rehnquist, the Court held that voir dire questions about the contents of the newspaper coverage to which jurors had been exposed were not constitutionally required.[49] Although such questions might be helpful in determining whether a prospective juror could be impartial, the key issue was the prospective juror's impartiality. As long as prospective jurors said that they could be impartial, and the trial judge found their assurances credible, they could be seated on the jury without violating the defendant's right to a fair trial. The Court be-

49. *Id.* at 425, 431–32.

lieved that the trial judge was in the best position to determine whether prospective jurors could be impartial. Unless the pretrial publicity reached the levels that it had in *Irvin v. Dowd*,[50] where many of those exposed said that they could not be impartial, the trial judge was not required by the Fourteenth Amendment to ask prospective jurors about the contents of the stories they had read in the newspapers. The dissent suggested that the trial judge needed to make a more searching inquiry in order to decide if prospective jurors could truly be impartial. Justice Marshall, writing for Justices Blackmun and Stevens, believed that at the very least, the trial judge needed to ask prospective jurors about which materials they had read, heard, or seen.[51] The trial judge was not to rely wholly upon the prospective juror's own assurances as to his or her impartiality. In addition, by asking these types of questions, the trial judge would be better able to assess the prospective juror's profession of impartiality. Justice Kennedy, also writing in dissent, would not limit the trial judge to a particular line of questioning, but would have the trial judge do more questioning than was done in this case and would have the trial judge question prospective jurors individually so that no prospective juror who had been exposed to pretrial publicity could be seated without assuring the court of his or her impartiality.[52]

50. 366 U.S. 717 (1961).

51. 500 U.S. at 438–39.

52. *Id.* at 450–52.

Policy Issues

The policy issues raised by voir dire include who should conduct the voir dire, whether prospective jurors should be questioned individually or collectively, when and how supplemental written questionnaires should be used, and how voir dire can elicit necessary and/or useful information from prospective jurors while still protecting their privacy and safety.

Judge- v. Attorney-Conducted Voir Dire. The question of who currently conducts the voir dire is answered differently depending on whether the parties are in federal or state court. In federal court, according to the Federal Rules, the judge may conduct the voir dire or have the parties or attorneys conduct the voir dire; this is so in civil and criminal cases.[53] If the judge conducts the voir dire, the attorneys or parties are permitted to supplement the judge's questions.[54] Although the Federal Rules provide that the judge or attorneys may conduct the voir dire, in practice, federal judges typically conduct the voir dire. In contrast, in some states, the attorneys conduct the voir dire, and they may even do so without the judge being present.[55]

Judges offer several reasons in support of judge-conducted voir dire. They explain that when they

53. *See* FED. R. CIV. P. 47(a); FED. R. CRIM. P. 24(a).

54. *See supra* note 53.

55. New York is an example of a state in which there is attorney-conducted voir dire. Until recently, judges did not even supervise the voir dire. As part of jury reform efforts initiated by

conduct voir dire, it proceeds quickly, does not intrude unnecessarily into prospective jurors' private lives, and allows questions to be asked in a neutral manner by a neutral arbiter. The main goal of voir dire is to uncover prospective jurors who cannot be impartial and judges believe that they accomplish this goal, whereas attorneys often have a different goal in mind: to identify prospective jurors who will be sympathetic to their case.

Most important, judge-conducted voir dire avoids the abuses of attorney-conducted voir dire. Judges believe that attorneys use voir dire for a variety of purposes, not all of them legitimate. Although attorneys are supposed to use voir dire to uncover biased jurors, or at least to exercise their peremptory challenges intelligently, they often use voir dire for other, less lofty, purposes, such as developing rapport with jurors, arguing their case to jurors, obtaining commitments from jurors, and trying to locate "friendly" jurors.

However, attorneys counter that they should be permitted to conduct voir dire as part of their zealous representation of their client. They argue that they alone are familiar with the case, know which questions to ask, and when to probe further with follow-up questions. They also complain that judges engage in only the most perfunctory questioning of prospective jurors, and as a result, this provides attorneys with little basis on which to exercise their peremptory challenges. In addition, if

Chief Judge Judith Kaye, however, judges now supervise the attorney-conducted voir dire in New York State courts.

they have little information about prospective jurors, then they are more likely to rely on "hunches" or stereotypes in selecting their jury. Some also have argued that voir dire is the only opportunity that a poor litigant has to learn about the jurors, whereas a rich litigant has other means, such as jury consultants, from which to glean information.[56]

In spite of attorneys' arguments, the trend is toward judge-conducted voir dire. At a time when judges in both federal and state courts face backlogs in their trial dockets, the attorney-conducted voir dire adds to the length of the trial and has been eliminated or curtailed in many jurisdictions in the name of efficiency.

Individual v. Group Voir Dire. The standard practice in both state and federal courts is to have the judge or attorney question prospective jurors as a group. This, too, is done in the name of efficiency. The practice is also done in the name of tradition because this is the way that voir dire has always been conducted in this country. In addition, the voir dire, like other stages of the trial, is open to the public, and by having a group voir dire in the courtroom, members of the public are free to observe it. Another advantage of a group voir dire, though perhaps an unintended one, is that prospective jurors have the opportunity to learn about each

56. *See, e.g.,* Barbara Allen Babcock, *Voir Dire: Preserving "Its Wonderful Power,"* 27 STAN. L. REV. 545, 558–59 (1975).

other. Those who are selected for the petit jury have learned about their fellow jurors' backgrounds and experiences as a result of having been questioned together.

There are several limitations, however, to a group voir dire. When prospective jurors are questioned as a group, individuals might not respond to questions, even if the questions are relevant to them. There are several reasons why they might remain silent: they are embarrassed to speak before a group; the information they have to offer is too private to say in a public setting; they worry that their response is socially unacceptable; they were confused by the question but did not wish to seek clarification in front of so many others and appear ignorant; they wish to deceive the parties and choose silence rather than outright deception.

In response to the above drawbacks, some judges have begun to experiment with some combination of group and individual voir dire. For one judge, this means inviting prospective jurors who wish to divulge personal information into the robing room— the judge's anteroom adjacent to the courtroom.[57]

57. *See* Kimba M. Wood, *The 1995 Justice Lester W. Roth Lecture: Reexamining the Access Doctrine*, 69 S. Cal. L. Rev. 1105, 1118–20 (1996).

Even though the prospective juror's response is given before the attorneys, judge, and court reporter, and is still part of the record, the smaller, more intimate setting of the robing room makes it easier to reveal such information. For another judge, this means conducting both a group and an individual voir dire in every case.[58] This judge found that the addition of an individual voir dire did not lengthen the voir dire process significantly and that it did allow him to uncover more germane information than a group voir dire alone provided. In particular, an individual voir dire means that no prospective juror can remain silent in response to a question. In this judge's experience, silence often masks essential information. This information, which only comes to light during the individual voir dire, might even provide a basis for excluding the prospective juror for cause.[59]

58. *See, e.g.*, Gregory E. Mize, *On Better Jury Selection: Spotting UFO Jurors Before They Enter the Jury Room*, COURT REV., Spring 1999, at 10.

59. Judge Mize offered numerous instances of prospective jurors who revealed information during the individual voir dire that they had not revealed during the group voir dire, and that this information led to their removal for cause. *Id.* at 12–13. For example, one prospective juror admitted to being the defendant's fiancée; another said that he had already lied during the voir

Written Questionnaires. Written question-naires, completed by prospective jurors while they wait in the Jury Assembly Room, provide back-ground information, particularly in high-profile cases. Although written questionnaires are not a substitute for the in-court voir dire, they allow the court and the attorneys to obtain background infor-mation about prospective jurors so that the in-court voir dire can focus primarily on their attitudes and individual views. Written questionnaires also can serve as an initial screen, revealing which prospec-tive jurors cannot be impartial in that case.

Currently, written questionnaires are not used in every case. This might be because they add time and cost to a case. Jury selection takes longer if attorneys first must agree on a written question-naire and then review the completed question-naires. The additional attorney hours also can add to the cost of a case. Attorneys also may resist a written questionnaire, even if it only supplements the in-court voir dire, because they distrust the answers that the prospective juror writes down or because they cannot see the prospective juror's de-meanor when he or she responds, as they can in the courtroom.

One question that is beginning to be raised is whether a written questionnaire can be completed quickly and inexpensively via the Internet. Some state courts have begun to move in this direction, though they still have a long way to go. A few

dire; yet another said that he did not understand the judge's questions and could not remember the past very well. *Id.* at 12.

courthouses, such as in Liberty County, Georgia, use a standard online questionnaire to determine whether a person is eligible to be summoned for jury duty.[60] Residents can complete the form at home on their computer, as long as their computer has an Internet connection, and they can submit it online. Other states, such as Massachusetts, provide a questionnaire online to elicit basic background information that prospective jurors can print at home, complete at their leisure, and bring to the courthouse on the day they report for jury service; otherwise, they can complete this questionnaire when they arrive at the courthouse.[61]

Although state courthouses have only begun to experiment with the Web, and are still far from creating a "Web voir dire," there are several advantages to a Web voir dire, even in an abbreviated form. It allows prospective jurors to respond to questions with care from the comfort of their homes and at their own convenience; it provides the parties and judge with basic background information about prospective jurors, thus allowing the in-court questioning to focus on prospective jurors' attitudes and views; it may lead to shorter, or at least to less tedious, in-court questioning; the results of the written questionnaires are easy to compile when

60. For an example of a questionnaire that is used to see if residents are eligible for jury duty, see Jury Qualification Questionnaire, *available at* http://www.libertyco.com/juryquest.htm (last visited Aug. 17, 2004).

61. *See* Confidential Jury Questionnaire, *available at* http://www.mass.gov/courts/jury/images/cFN-new2.jpg (last visited Aug. 17, 2004).

they are submitted by computer; the questions may seem less intrusive to prospective jurors when they are presented in written form, even though the written questions and answers are still part of the record; and when the prospective jurors' responses are made public, their names do not have to be attached to the questionnaires, thus giving prospective jurors a little more privacy than they would have when that information is revealed in the courtroom.

Like all innovations, Web voir dire is likely to meet with some resistance. Some prospective jurors may resist either because they are uncomfortable with computers or because they do not have easy access to them. However, for such prospective jurors (and the numbers will dwindle over time), alternate means of submitting a written questionnaire could be made available. Some lawyers also may resist because they worry that they will be sacrificing face-to-face questions for written questions, even though a written questionnaire is intended to supplement, and not to supplant, in-court voir dire. Some judges also may resist because they worry that a new way of conducting voir dire could raise constitutional issues that are as yet unanticipated. They also are accustomed to conducting voir dire in a certain way and any change not only runs counter to their practice, but also invites appellate court review. With appellate review, there is always the chance that the higher court may reject the new procedure.

Protecting Juror Privacy and Safety. One way in which courts try to protect juror privacy is to limit the questions that are asked during voir dire. Judges claim that questions should not be overly intrusive or jurors will resent the invasion of their privacy.[62] In contrast, lawyers argue that the voir dire is too cursory and that they need to worry more about eliciting information from prospective jurors and less about protecting juror privacy.

When federal judges, for example, conduct a voir dire, their inquiry tends to be limited to such basic information as the general area where the juror lives, his or her occupation, marital status, whether the juror has a spouse or children, and, if so, their occupations. The judge is trying to discern whether there are any obvious reasons why that prospective juror cannot serve. The catch-all question that the judge will typically ask is whether the prospective juror believes he or she can be impartial. Once the prospective juror has answered that question in the affirmative, that usually signals the end of the questioning for the juror. Judges leave it up to the prospective juror to decide whether he or she can be impartial; attorneys are less willing to accept the prospective juror's self-assessment and are more willing than the judge to push the inquiry further. For example, lawyers have sometimes wanted to ask

62. *But see* Mary R. Rose, *A Voir Dire of Voir Dire: Listening to Jurors' Views Regarding the Peremptory Challenge,* 78 CHI.-KENT L. REV. 1061 (2003) (questioning jurors serving in North Carolina and finding that they did not resent lawyers' questions during voir dire and understood that it was part of the jury selection process).

prospective jurors about their religion or sexual orientation during voir dire, but judges have usually denied such inquiries on the ground that it is an intrusion into the juror's privacy and not necessary for the parties to know.[63]

One way in which courts have attempted to protect juror safety is by seating an "anonymous jury." With an anonymous jury, the judge and lawyers refer to prospective jurors by their given name or assigned juror number during the voir dire. Their complete names are kept sealed throughout jury selection, the trial, and sometimes even after a verdict has been rendered. This practice has typically been limited to high-profile cases or cases in which there is a particular reason to worry about juror safety, such as cases involving gang members, drug dealers, or organized crime. At least one academic has urged that this practice be adhered to in all cases so as not to create fear among jurors in certain kinds of cases that will lead them to prejudge the defendant.[64]

The California legislature has passed legislation that comes close to this practice in criminal cases in

63. *See, e.g.*, United States v. Greer, 939 F.2d 1076 (5th Cir. 1991) (affirming a trial judge's refusal to exclude Jewish and Latino jurors for cause and refusal to require prospective jurors to reveal whether they were Jewish); People v. Garcia, 77 Cal. App.4th 1269, 1281 (Ct. App. 2000) ("The whole point is that no one can be excluded because of sexual orientation. That being the case, no one should be allowed to inquire about it.").

64. *See* Nancy J. King, *Nameless Justice: The Case for the Routine Use of Anonymous Juries in Criminal Trials*, 49 VAND. L. REV. 123 (1996).

California. California judges use "confidential juries," in which "names and identifying information are withheld even after a verdict, but the names are shown to the lawyers during jury selection."[65] This practice, which has been upheld on appeal, was motivated by concerns for juror safety and privacy. Anonymous juries and confidential juries, designed to allay juror fears, are in tension with the interests of defendants. Defendants are likely to argue that such practices deny them a truly public trial, insofar as the jurors are not identified to the public, and that the jurors themselves might feel less accountable for their verdict because their identities are never disclosed.

Peremptory Challenges

Peremptory challenges are the challenges that lawyers exercise to remove prospective jurors from the panel without, at least traditionally, having to explain why. Although the peremptory challenge is not required by the U.S. Constitution, it always has been part of our jury tradition in both civil and criminal cases. The other means of removing a prospective juror from a panel is with a for cause challenge. This challenge is typically reserved for prospective jurors who are related to a participant in the trial, who have a financial interest in the outcome of the case, or who say they cannot be impartial. Judges have discretion to grant for cause challenges. Although there is no fixed number, judges are usually restrained in granting a for cause

65. Jerry Markon, *Judges Pushing for More Privacy of Jurors' Names*, WALL ST. J., June 27, 2001, at B1.

challenge, perhaps because they know that peremptory challenges are available. In contrast, lawyers decide whether to exercise a peremptory challenge and they have only a specified number of peremptories to exercise.

One benefit of the peremptory challenge is that it assures parties that they can remove those prospective jurors about whom they have misgivings, even if they cannot articulate exactly why. With the traditional peremptory, they need not give any reason at all. Another benefit is that the peremptory challenge allows parties to participate in the selection of their jury. The idea is that the parties will feel more comfortable with a jury that they have chosen rather than with one chosen by the judge.

A Key Legal Issue: To Which Groups Does Equal Protection Apply?

Although the peremptory challenge has always been part of our jury tradition and has provided certain benefits, it also has provided a vehicle by which some prospective jurors were struck because of their race or some other group characteristic. When no reason had to be given, attorneys were free to use peremptories in a discriminatory manner. This often took the form of exercising peremptories to exclude African-American men, and later women, from serving on a petit jury.

The issue of race-based peremptory challenges was first addressed by the Supreme Court in *Swain v. Alabama*.[66] There, petitioner Swain, an African-

66. 380 U.S. 202 (1965).

American man, claimed that the prosecutor's use of peremptory challenges to remove from the venire all six African-American men violated the Equal Protection Clause of the Fourteenth Amendment. His argument was that whereas white defendants could be tried by a jury drawn from a venire that included whites, he, an African-American, could only be tried by a jury from which members of his race had been excluded from the venire in a racially discriminatory manner. The Court, after recounting the history of the peremptory challenge and its integral role in the American jury system, held that Swain had not established that the prosecutor had exercised his peremptory challenges in a discriminatory manner. The Court explained that in order for Swain to establish such a violation, he would have to show that, in case after case, the prosecutor had exercised his peremptories against African-Americans because of their race. In *Swain*, the Court little realized that it had created "a crippling burden of proof"[67] for a defendant seeking to establish that the prosecution had engaged in discriminatory peremptories.

Over twenty-five years later, when the Supreme Court revisited the issue in *Batson v. Kentucky*,[68] it acknowledged that the evidentiary burden it had created in *Swain* was too onerous.[69] As a result, prosecutors had continued to exercise peremptories in a discriminatory manner and defendants were

67. Batson v. Kentucky, 476 U.S. 79, 92 (1986).

68. *Id.* at 79.

69. *Id.* at 93.

hard-pressed to stop them. Justice Powell, writing for the Court in *Batson*, tried to strike a delicate balance. The Court wanted both to preserve the peremptory challenge and yet to halt the exercise of racially discriminatory peremptories. The Court created in *Batson* what has come to be called "the modified peremptory challenge," or what Chief Justice Burger described in his dissent in *Batson* as "a curious hybrid."[70]

If a defendant can establish a prima facie case of a racially discriminatory peremptory, then the prosecution must give a reason for the exercise of that peremptory challenge. Although the defining feature of the peremptory had always been that no reason had to be given for its exercise, after *Batson*, that was no longer the case. To establish a prima facie case, the defendant must show that he is a member of the racial group that has been discriminated against; that peremptories permit " 'those to discriminate who are of a mind to discriminate;' " and that these and other facts raise an inference that the prosecutor has used his peremptories to strike prospective jurors based on their race.[71]

After the defendant has established a prima facie case of a racially discriminatory peremptory (step one), the burden then shifts to the prosecutor to come forward with a race-neutral reason for the strike (step two). Although the prosecutor's reason need not rise to the level required of a for cause

70. *Id.* at 126.
71. *Id.* at 96.

challenge,[72] it is not sufficient for the prosecutor to say that his peremptory was based on hunch, intuition, or the assumption that all African Americans are likely to view a case in a certain way.[73] If the judge finds the prosecutor's reason to be race-neutral, the peremptory will be permitted; if the judge finds the reason to be pretextual, the peremptory will be prohibited (step three).

With *Batson*, the Court created an uneasy compromise. It preserved the peremptory challenge, even though some peremptories now require reasons. It also overruled the evidentiary burden of proof required by *Swain*. No longer does a defendant have to gather statistics about a prosecutor's exercise of peremptories in past cases. Instead, a defendant is free to rely on the prosecutor's exercise of peremptories in defendant's case alone.

Batson also created an elaborate structure by which a defendant can object to the prosecutor's peremptories. Although the requirement that the defendant establish a prima facie case meant that only a limited number of peremptory challenges would require reasons, some critics, like Chief Justice Burger, worried that *Batson* had forever changed the nature of the peremptory. He warned that *Batson* had done this by requiring reasons when the very nature of a peremptory challenge is that no reason need be given,[74] and it had opened

72. *Id.* at 97.

73. 476 U.S. at 97.

74. *Id.* at 127 (Burger, C.J., dissenting) ("Analytically, there is no middle ground: A challenge either has to be explained or it

the door to members of other groups who also might claim that prosecutors had used peremptories to discriminate against them. Chief Justice Burger feared that there would be no logical stopping point once the door had been opened to challenges to the peremptory challenge. Eventually, reasons would have to be given not just for peremptories based on race, but also for those based on gender and other group characteristics, and not only when objections were raised by defendants, but also by prosecutors.[75]

Although Chief Justice Burger's dire prediction of the demise of the peremptory challenge has not yet come to pass, he was correct in surmising that the modified peremptory would be expanded. In a line of cases since *Batson*, the Court has expanded the reach of *Batson*. In *Powers v. Ohio*,[76] the Court extended *Batson* challenges to enable white criminal defendants to object to the exercise of prosecutorial peremptories directed against African Americans. The Court, in an opinion by Justice Kennedy, reasoned that the harms to the litigant, to the excluded juror, and to the community were no less significant regardless of the race of the defendant.[77] Through the doctrine of third-party standing, petitioner Powers was permitted to raise a *Batson* challenge on behalf of those prospective jurors who were

does not.... [T]o permit inquiry into the basis for a peremptory challenge would force 'the peremptory challenge [to] collapse into the challenge for cause.' ") (citation omitted).

75. *Id.* at 124, 126.
76. 499 U.S. 400 (1991).
77. *Id.* at 406.

excluded by the prosecution by virtue of their race.[78] When the question of racially discriminatory peremptories arose in the civil context in *Edmonson v. Leesville Concrete Co.*,[79] the logic of *Batson* also prevailed. The Court held that civil litigants, when engaged in the exercise of peremptory challenges, were temporarily state actors, and were under the same obligation as prosecutors to avoid race-based peremptory challenges. When the question whether a criminal defendant could engage in race-based peremptories arose in *Georgia v. McCollum*,[80] the Court held that the criminal defendant, like the prosecutor, was precluded by the Fourteenth Amendment from exercising racially discriminatory peremptories.

The prohibition of discriminatory peremptory challenges was not limited to race, but eventually included gender. In *J.E.B. v. Alabama ex rel. T.B.*,[81] the State of Alabama, on behalf of the mother of a minor child, sought to establish the paternity of the child. The putative father challenged the State's exercise of nine of its ten peremptory challenges to remove male prospective jurors. Petitioner claimed that the State's exercise of peremptories on the basis of gender violated the Fourteenth Amendment's Equal Protection Clause, and the Supreme Court agreed. The Court, after comparing women's history of discrimination to African Americans' his-

78. *Id.* at 415.

79. 500 U.S. 614 (1991).

80. 505 U.S. 42 (1992).

81. 511 U.S. 127 (1994).

tory, decided that it need not determine which history had led to greater suffering; all that it needed to examine under the "heightened scrutiny" afforded all gender classifications was whether the state had " 'an exceedingly persuasive justification' " for its gender-based classifications.[82] The Court concluded that Alabama did not have an exceedingly persuasive justification for its gender-based peremptories; in fact, the State's rationale—that men were more likely to be sympathetic to a man's arguments in a paternity suit—was based on "gross generalizations" and stereotypes that would be impermissible in the context of race and should likewise be impermissible in the context of gender. Once again, those in dissent raised the spectre of the demise of the peremptory. Justice Scalia, joined by Chief Justice Rehnquist and Justice Thomas, echoed Chief Justice Burger's lament in *Batson*, observing that "much damage has been done. It has been done, first and foremost, to the peremptory challenge system, which loses its whole character when ... 'reasons' for strikes must be given."[83] Justice Scalia, like the former Chief Justice, also predicted that it would not be long before the " 'reasoned peremptory' " would extend beyond race and gender to include other groups as well.[84]

Although Justice Scalia and Chief Justice Burger saw no logical stopping point, the Court has been

82. *Id.* at 136 (quoting Personnel Admin. of Mass. v. Feeney, 442 U.S. 256 (1979)).

83. *Id.* at 161.

84. *Id.* at 162.

hesitant to extend the modified peremptory beyond race, ethnicity,[85] and gender. When given the opportunity to consider whether peremptories based on religion violate the Equal Protection Clause, the Court declined, and denied the petition for a writ of certiorari.[86] Justices Thomas and Scalia, who had dissented in *J.E.B.*, dissented from the denial of certiorari in *Davis v. Minnesota*, claiming that if the Court were serious about its principles, it should have granted certiorari in *Davis*.

In *Davis*, the Minnesota Supreme Court had interpreted *Batson* to be limited to race, and not to extend to religion. Since the Court had extended *Batson* beyond race in *J.E.B.*, Justices Thomas and Scalia believed that the Court should have granted, vacated, and remanded the petition in *Davis* so that the Minnesota Supreme Court could consider religious-based peremptories in light of the Court's decision in *J.E.B.* The reasoning of the two dissenting justices was that since *J.E.B.* further contributed to the demise of the peremptory by opening it to challenge by any group protected not just by strict scrutiny, as is the case with racial classifications, but to intermediate or heightened scrutiny, as is the

85. Hernandez v. New York, 500 U.S. 352 (1991). Although the Court held that peremptory challenges exercised against Spanish-speaking prospective jurors did not violate the Equal Protection Clause in this particular case, the Court recognized that ethnicity was a protected category under the Fourteenth Amendment and that peremptories could not be exercised on the basis of ethnicity.

86. Davis v. Minnesota, 511 U.S. 1115 (1994).

case with gender-based classifications, then religious-based peremptories also must be open to challenge. In dissenting from the denial of certiorari, Justices Thomas and Scalia tried to highlight that the road from *Batson* to *J.E.B.* led to the end of the peremptory challenge.

For the Court, however, the road from *Batson* to *J.E.B.* has not led inexorably to the end of the peremptory challenge. The Court has remained steadfast in its commitment to both the peremptory challenge and a nondiscriminatory jury selection process. The *Batson* progeny—*Powers*, *Edmonson*, and *McCollum*—are a testament to both commitments. What is striking about this development, however, is not the Court's commitment to the peremptory, which has been longstanding, but its commitment to nondiscriminatory jury selection, which is not only recent but seems likely to outweigh its commitment to the peremptory if it were forced to choose.

The only point at which the Court began to waiver in its commitment to nondiscriminatory peremptory challenges was in a little noticed *per curiam* opinion in a case called *Purkett v. Elem*.[87] In *Elem*, the criminal defendant, an African-American man, objected to the prosecutor's use of peremptory challenges to strike two African-American men from the panel. The prosecutor provided reasons for his strikes, which in the case of one prospective juror was because of his long hair, mustache and goatee, and which in the case of the other was

87. 514 U.S. 765 (1995).

because of his mustache and goatee.[88] The prosecutor added that the second prospective juror had once been the victim of a supermarket robbery at which a sawed-off shotgun had been pointed at him and so he might expect that a robbery required a gun, and there was no gun in this case of second-degree robbery. The trial judge overruled the defendant's objections and the Missouri Court of Appeals affirmed. When defendant raised the claim in his habeas petition, the district court judge denied it, but the Eighth Circuit reversed and remanded as to the first prospective juror, explaining that the reasons had not been plausibly race-neutral.

The Supreme Court reversed and remanded, explaining that at the second step of the inquiry—when the prosecutor must provide a race-neutral explanation for his strike—the explanation need not be persuasive or even plausible; it simply must be race-neutral. The Supreme Court concluded that the Eighth Circuit had erred by combining the second and third steps, thus requiring not only a race-neutral explanation, but also a persuasive one. The Court, by allowing reasons no matter how silly or implausible as long as they are nondiscriminatory, has begun for the first time to undermine the force of *Batson*. Justice Stevens, writing in dissent, noted that in *Elem* the Court had quietly replaced *Batson*'s more rigorous standard of a reason that is "related to the particular case to be tried"[89] with a more lax one in which any neutral explanation, "no

88. *Id.* at 766.

89. Batson v. Kentucky, 476 U.S. 79, 98 (1986).

matter how 'implausible or fantastic' " or " 'silly or superstitious' " would be sufficient to rebut a prima facie case of discrimination.[90]

Policy Issue: What To Do About the Peremptory?

Although the case law on peremptory challenges may appear labyrinthine, there are several points on which it is clear. First, peremptory challenges cannot be exercised on the basis of race, ethnicity, and gender. The Equal Protection Clause of the Fourteenth Amendment prohibits such discriminatory peremptories, whether they are exercised in civil or criminal cases, by defendants or prosecutors, or by whites or blacks. Second, the Court is committed both to preserving the peremptory challenge and to prohibiting discrimination during jury selection. These two goals appear to be on a collision course: the Court cannot continue to add to the number of groups protected from discriminatory peremptories without, at some point, eliminating the peremptory challenge altogether. However, the Court has proceeded slowly and cautiously, and has not yet reached that collision point. Third, the three-part test delineated in *Batson*, in which the defendant must establish a prima facie case of discriminatory peremptories, the prosecutor must then provide a race-neutral explanation, and the trial judge must assess whether the reason given is pretextual, has provided a cumbersome mechanism for evaluating peremptory challenges. Although this mechanism is the one currently in force, it is not without its limitations, as a matter of policy.

90. 514 U.S. at 775.

The *Batson* approach to peremptory challenges, although laudable in its goal to eliminate discrimination from jury selection, has several limitations, some of which have only become clear over time. One limitation is that those who are of a mind to discriminate can continue to do so; they simply need to couch their impermissible reasons in race- or gender-neutral language. This limitation has become even more pronounced now that the reasons no longer have to bear any connection to the case. A second limitation is that the reasons accepted by one trial judge as race-neutral may be rejected by another trial judge as pretextual, thus leading to inconsistencies among trial courts and uncertainties for litigants. A third limitation is that the *Batson* structure has added an extra layer of hearings to jury selection. Any time there is a *Batson* challenge, the judge must arrange for a sidebar or a mini-hearing outside the presence of the prospective jurors in order to hear the objections and decide whether a prima facie case has been established. If so established, the trial judge will have to evaluate the other side's reasons and decide whether they are race-neutral, and ultimately, nonpretextual. Fourth, appellate courts tend to be quite deferential to the trial judge's decision in a *Batson* challenge. The trial judge can assess the demeanor of the prospective jurors and the attorneys, whereas the appellate judges have only the cold record before them. As a result, even though the trial judge's decision is subject to appellate review, it is very hard to disturb the trial judge's ruling. Parties may think they have been given several levels of protection, but in fact, a *Batson* challenge often begins and ends with the trial judge.

In light of the limitations of *Batson*, many jury scholars, judges, and even some practitioners have wondered whether there is a better way to proceed with or without peremptory challenges. At one end of the debate are those who would eliminate the peremptory challenge. Justice Marshall, in his concurrence in *Batson*, was one of the early advocates of this position.[91] In his view, as long as there are peremptory challenges, they will be used as a vehicle for discrimination during jury selection. He did not see any way to rid jury selection of discrimination while preserving the peremptory challenge because discriminatory motives could be conscious as well as unconscious.[92] Several other judges, such as Constance Baker-Motley in the Southern District of New York[93] and Morris Hoffman in the Second Judicial District of Colorado,[94] as well as a number of legal academics,[95] adhere to Justice Marshall's view about the peremptory.

91. 476 U.S. 79, 102 (1986) (Marshall, J., concurring).

92. *Id.* at 106.

93. Minetos v. City Univ., 925 F.Supp. 177, 185 (S.D.N.Y. 1996) ("It is time to put an end to this charade. We have now had enough judicial experience with the *Batson* test to know that it does not truly unmask discrimination.").

94. Morris B. Hoffman, *Peremptory Challenges Should Be Abolished: A Trial Judge's Perspective*, 64 U. CHI. L. REV. 809, 810, 850 (1997).

95. *See, e.g.*, ABRAMSON, *supra* note 3 (Ch. 2), at 137–39; Nancy S. Marder, *Beyond Gender: Peremptory Challenges and*

The elimination of the peremptory challenge raises the loudest objections from defense attorneys
who believe that criminal defendants have a right,
as a matter of tradition, if not of constitutional
guarantee, to exercise peremptory challenges. They
worry that without peremptories, prospective jurors
who cannot be impartial will be seated on the petit
jury because judges are not always generous about
granting for cause challenges. Many attorneys also
believe that part of their trial skill consists of selecting a sympathetic jury (though parties do not have
a right to a sympathetic jury). Without peremptory
challenges, these attorneys believe their clients
would lose an advantage that they could otherwise
give them.

A more incremental approach to the peremptory
is to limit the number of peremptories available to
each side.[96] The reasoning behind this approach is
that even if attorneys manage to use their peremptories in a discriminatory manner, if they have
fewer peremptories available to them, then they are
not going to be able to eliminate all of the minorities or all of the women on the venire. This approach would ease the fears of defense attorneys,
but would not satisfy those, like Justice Marshall,
who believe that there is no place in the courtroom
for discrimination even if it is done on a limited
basis.

the Roles of the Jury, 73 TEX. L. REV. 1041, 1044–47, 1052–86,
1095–99 (1995).

96. *See* Jean Montoya, *The Future of the Post-*Batson *Peremptory Challenge: Voir Dire by Questionnaire and the "Blind"
Peremptory,* 29 U. MICH. J.L. REFORM 981, 1011 & n.144 (1996)
(citing scholars and commentators who have made this proposal).

A more creative, though perhaps less realistic, approach recommended by one academic is to have "blind peremptories."[97] Attorneys still would be able to exercise peremptory challenges, but they would not be able to see the prospective jurors. The information about the prospective jurors would be provided by written questionnaire. The theory is that if they could not see the gender, race, ethnicity, or other characteristics of the prospective juror, then they could not use those impermissible categories as a basis for striking that prospective juror. Without the visual cues, attorneys would simply have to rely on the responses that the prospective juror gave to the questionnaire. Attorneys would have to exercise their peremptory challenges based on the individual attitudes or views revealed in the questionnaire, rather than on any stereotypical beliefs they hold. However, this approach might run afoul of the Sixth Amendment because criminal defendants could argue that they have a right to "an impartial jury" and that they cannot be assured an impartial jury if they are unable to see their jury during the selection process. Without face-to-face questioning, an attorney might miss valuable visual cues and fail to strike a prospective juror who could not be impartial.

Although a number of states' jury reform commissions have considered whether peremptory challenges should be eliminated, reduced in number, or revised in some other way, most have recommended

97. *Id.* at 1015–16.

that their states simply maintain the status quo
with respect to peremptory challenges.[98]

Practical Matters

Number of Peremptories. Each party has the
option of exercising a certain number of peremptories, and the number varies, depending upon whether the case is in state or federal court or is civil or
criminal in nature. For example, in federal court in
a civil case, each side can exercise three peremptory
challenges.[99] In federal court in a criminal case, the
number varies, based upon the potential punishment. In a case punishable by death, both the
government and the defendant each have twenty
peremptory challenges.[100] In a case punishable by
imprisonment of not more than one year or a fine
or both, each side is entitled to three peremptory
challenges.[101] For cause challenges, unlike peremptory challenges, are not limited to any particular
number in a given trial; they are, however, left to
the trial judge's discretion.

98.   *See, e.g.*, THE POWER OF 12, *supra* note 39 (Ch. 3), at 68–69.

99.   *See* FED. R. CIV. P. 47(b) ("The court shall allow the
number of peremptory challenges provided by 28 U.S.C.
§ 1870."); 28 U.S.C. § 1870 ("In civil cases, each party shall be
entitled to three peremptory challenges.").

100.   *See* FED. R. CRIM. P. 24(b).

101.   *See id.*

Making an Objection. When a party has exercised one or more than one of its peremptories in a
manner that suggests it might have been motivated
by discrimination, it is up to the other side to raise
a *Batson* challenge. To do this, an objection must be
made immediately, and certainly before the petit
jury has been empanelled. The party making the
Batson challenge should be sure to set forth on the
record the facts that suggest that the peremptory
was discriminatory, including the race, gender or
ethnicity of the prospective juror who has been
struck peremptorily. Although a pattern of peremptories exercised against members of a particular
race, gender, or ethnicity would help to make the
case, a pattern is *not* necessary; a single peremptory
challenge can be the basis of a *Batson* challenge.

Role of Jury Consultants. One of the ways in
which trial attorneys rely on jury consultants is in
the selection of a jury.[102] A jury consultant can
assist an attorney in formulating open-ended questions for the voir dire and can help an attorney in
selecting jurors that the consultant believes will
favor the attorney's case. In helping the attorney to

102. Another way is that jury consultants arrange for mock
juries to hear the attorneys' arguments in preparation for trial.
By observing the mock jurors' deliberations and by questioning
the mock jurors afterward, consultants can advise attorneys on
the most effective arguments.

select jurors, the consultant might advise the attorney on the exercise of peremptory challenges. The role of the jury consultant should raise a number of issues for courts.

One issue is whether the jury consultant ought to be constrained by *Batson* and its progeny in the same ways that an attorney is. An attorney is said to be a state actor for purposes of jury selection who cannot engage in discriminatory peremptories that violate the Fourteenth Amendment. Is a jury consultant a state actor for purposes of jury selection? If so, then a jury consultant cannot engage in group-based assumptions about how jurors might vote. If not, then what should courts do about jury consultants who advise attorneys to engage in group-based assumptions about prospective jurors that violate *Batson*? Of course, such knowledge may never reach the court because attorneys could frame the reasons for the peremptory challenge in race- or gender-neutral language, but what if the peremptory is motivated by the consultant's impermissible group-based assumptions? Are jury consultants a convenient way for attorneys to circumvent the strictures of *Batson*? Can they simply attribute the impermissible stereotypical thinking to their jury consultant rather than taking responsibility for it themselves?

A second issue is whether there are any regulations to which a jury consultant should be subject during jury selection. An attorney is an officer of the court; a jury consultant is not. An attorney is a member of a bar; a jury consultant is not. Each of these affiliations imposes restraints on an attorney to act in accordance with the rules of the court; a jury consultant may feel no such compunction.

A third issue is whether jury consultants should be permitted to assist in jury selection or whether they increase the disparity between rich and poor litigants in a process that is supposed to be fair and to set the tone for the entire trial. One of the justifications for eliminating discriminatory peremptories was that the court announces each peremptory challenge as it is made; in other words, the selection process appears to receive the imprimatur of the court.[103] The Supreme Court recognized that when courts permitted discriminatory peremptories, they undermined the integrity of their own proceedings. In the exercise of peremptory challenges and the selection of the jury, which take place under the auspices of the court and under the watchful gaze of the public, should rich litigants have an ostensible advantage over poor litigants by having the assistance of jury consultants?

103. Powers v. Ohio, 499 U.S. 400 (1991).

The role of the jury consultant in jury selection in general and in the exercise of peremptory challenges in particular is uncharted territory. There are no rules, court-imposed or otherwise, governing jury consultants' participation at this stage of the trial proceedings. If the goal of *Batson*—to root out discrimination during jury selection—is ever to be achieved, it seems that *Batson* should extend to jury consultants and the advice they give to attorneys in exercising peremptory challenges, even though there are no rules in place at this time to ensure that this occurs.

CHAPTER 6

JURY TRIAL ISSUES

The traditional view of the juror's role throughout the trial is that of an empty vessel into which information, presented in the form of exhibits, testimony, argument, and judicial instructions, will be poured. Another way to understand this traditional conception is to think of the juror as a sponge. In other words, the juror will simply absorb all of the information presented at trial, just as a sponge absorbs water. According to this view, jurors will be able to retain all of the trial information until they are ready to discuss it during jury deliberations.

One judge has described this traditional view of the juror as "the passive juror," and has recommended that it be replaced with another view: "the active juror."[1] The model of the active juror recognizes that jurors need to be engaged in learning throughout the trial, just as students need to be engaged in learning throughout a course, and not just at the end.[2] The active juror, like the active student, is able to process information as it is presented, to ask questions when he or she is confused, and to begin to organize and to analyze the

1. *See* Dann, *supra* note 38 (Ch. 3), at 1240–47.
2. *Id.*

105

information throughout the trial process, and not just during deliberations.[3]

There are a number of tools that jurors could use during the trial that would enhance their ability to retain, understand, and analyze the information during their deliberations. Whether jurors should play an active or passive role during the trial is a matter of debate among judges, lawyers, and academics. My own view is that the active juror model reflects more accurately how people learn, and should lead to giving jurors additional tools to perform their roles more effectively. However, even those judges and lawyers who do not espouse the active juror model still might be willing to give jurors some tools that will help them to perform their job more competently. Judging from current court practices, there has been a move toward allowing jurors to take notes during the trial. In contrast, there has been reluctance to allow jurors to submit written questions to the judge during

3. A brief film, produced by the Institute of the International Association of Defense Counsel (IADC) Foundation, contrasts the two competing conceptions of the juror's proper role during trial by showing what would happen if students were asked to learn in the same way that jurors are. *See* Videotape: Order in the Classroom (Institute of the IADC Foundation 1998). In the film, students are told that their academic course will be run according to the rules of a jury: they will not be able to take notes, ask questions, know the subject matter of the course, or even discuss the material until the end of the course, at which point they must all agree on the answer for the final exam; they all will receive the same grade; and they will never know if they reached the right answer. Their looks of bewilderment, frustration, and disbelief suggest how jurors must feel when confronted with the role they are traditionally asked to play during a trial.

trial and to permit jurors to exchange views during the trial, rather than waiting until the deliberations have formally begun.

Juror Note-Taking

One tool that has gained some acceptance among judges and lawyers is juror note-taking during the trial. Traditionally, jurors were not permitted to take notes. There are a number of justifications for this prohibition, though its origin is difficult to discern.[4] One concern is that if jurors took copious notes, then they might miss some crucial aspect of a witness's demeanor. A witness's demeanor is one of the ways that jurors are to judge witness credibility, which is, after all, part of the jury's fact-finding role. A second concern is that note-taking might be a source of distraction. Jurors might use note-taking as an excuse to doodle or otherwise fail to focus on the trial. A third problem is how jurors would use their notes during the deliberations. Would jurors rely on their notes, however faulty they might be, rather than requesting exhibits or read-

4. One explanation is that originally most jurors were illiterate. Thus, there was a general prohibition on note-taking because few jurors could actually take notes and courts did not want to give an advantage to the few jurors who could. *See* Larry Heurer & Steven Penrod, *Juror Notetaking and Question Asking During Trials*, 18 LAW & HUM. BEHAV. 121, 124 (1994) ("The concern [with juror note-taking] was that if a single juror could read the materials, that juror would be inordinately persuasive with his illiterate fellow jurors."). This early justification, however, has little bearing on today's jurors who are statutorily required to be able to write in English in order to be considered qualified to serve, at least in federal court. *See* 28 U.S.C. § 1865(b)(2).

backs of testimony? Would jurors who took extensive notes be more highly regarded, and therefore
more persuasive, than jurors who took minimal
notes? Finally, there is the question of what to do
with the notes once the jury had rendered a verdict.
Could jurors' notes be used to challenge a verdict?
Would they be made available to attorneys?

In spite of these concerns and questions, there
has been a trend toward allowing jurors to take
notes.[5] One reason to permit juror note-taking is
that it is likely to enhance juror recollection, particularly in lengthy or complex cases. A second reason
is that note-taking might actually encourage jurors
to pay close attention to the trial; note-taking focuses jurors' attention on what is taking place in the
courtroom. A third reason is that it allows jurors to
organize the tremendous amount of material that is
presented at trial, without having to wait until the
end of the trial to do so. Finally, some jurors might
be less inclined to participate in deliberations because they have less confidence in their recollections, particularly when other jurors are recalling
the testimony or exhibits in a different way. If these
jurors have recourse to their notes, however, they
might be more inclined to voice their views and this

5. One book published in 1997 described the practice of juror
note-taking as "widespread." JURY TRIAL INNOVATIONS, *supra* note
22 (Ch. 5), at 141. Ten years earlier, however, an Administrative
Office of the U.S. Courts' estimate had indicated that "90
percent of the federal judges do *not* permit jurors to take notes."
SAUL KASSIN & LAWRENCE WRIGHTSMAN, THE AMERICAN JURY ON TRIAL
128 (1988). Thus, in just a decade, the practice became far more
prevalent than ever before.

will give the jury more information to consider during its deliberations.

Whether jurors are permitted to take notes during trial is usually a matter left to the discretion of the trial court.[6] In those jurisdictions in which such discretion is not provided by statute or rule, the parties can agree to allow juror note-taking.[7] Numerous commentators have urged judges to allow juror note-taking. For example, the American Bar Association and Brookings Institution compiled a report after their symposium on the civil jury in which they described juror note-taking as "the most widely suggested reform for enhancing juror comprehension" and recommended that courts adopt it.[8] Indeed, according to two studies, when judges and lawyers actually have experience with note-taking, they tend to view it favorably.[9] In sum, although juror note-taking is not uniformly permitted and remains largely within the trial judge's discretion, the practice has become more widespread, and in those courtrooms in which it has been tried, judges, lawyers, and jurors have responded favorably.

6. JURY TRIAL INNOVATIONS, *supra* note 22 (Ch. 5), at 141 ("In most jurisdictions, the trial judge has discretion to permit jurors to take notes.").

7. *Id.*

8. ABA/BROOKINGS SYMPOSIUM, CHARTING A FUTURE FOR THE CIVIL JURY SYSTEM 18 (1992).

9. *See, e.g.*, Heurer & Penrod, *supra* note 4, at 140; Leonard B. Sand & Steven Alan Reiss, *A Report on Seven Experiments Conducted by District Court Judges in the Second Circuit*, 60 N.Y.U. L. REV. 423, 446–52 (1985).

Those judges who have permitted jurors to take notes also have found that most of the practical concerns can be allayed through judicial instructions. For example, judges can instruct jurors that they can take notes, but that they need not take notes (so that those who choose not to take notes do not feel that they are shirking their responsibilities). In addition, judges can caution jurors to pay close attention to the witnesses when they testify and not to allow their note-taking to interfere with their observations. Judges also can instruct the jury that it can request exhibits and read-backs of testimony during the deliberations and that jurors need not rely wholly upon their notes or recollections. Finally, judges who allow note-taking should provide notepads and pens to all the jurors at the start of the trial. At the end of the trial, after the jury has rendered its verdict, the court can collect the notes and destroy them so that they serve solely as an aid to jurors and are not used for any other purpose.

Juror Questions

Another tool that courts can give jurors during the trial to enhance their comprehension of the proceedings is the opportunity to ask questions. Although the spectre of jurors raising their hands or calling out their questions any time during the trial would certainly cause discomfort to lawyers and judges alike, the way in which jurors ask questions in practice is actually far less disruptive. In those courtrooms that have experimented with juror questions, the preferred method is to have jurors submit their questions unsigned and in writing to the judge. The judge can then decide, usually in consultation with the lawyers, which questions either the judge or lawyers will answer. If the question is one that is inappropriate for either to address, the judge can simply explain this to the jury. By having the question submitted in writing, the judge and lawyers control when jurors ask their questions; they also have time for well-considered answers.

In spite of such controls, juror questions have met with resistance from lawyers and judges. Lawyers object to jurors asking questions because they want to be in control of their trial presentation. They worry that if jurors ask questions—even in written form—such questions still might interrupt the flow of the trial. They also worry that the question a juror asks might be on an issue that they intentionally and strategically chose not to raise. Even if the judge explained to the jury why a particular question could not be answered, lawyers still worry that the juror with the question might resent the lawyers' lack of response. Finally, lawyers worry that jurors, in being permitted to ask questions, might be too quick to make judgments before they have heard both sides' presentations and that they might become more like advocates for their own position than neutral fact-finders.

Judges also worry about the practice of jurors asking questions. They want to be in control of the courtroom, and a practice such as juror questions, which can add an element of unpredictability to the proceedings, is unwelcome from their vantage point. In addition, judges, who face backlogged dockets, are reluctant to add a practice that could lengthen trials. They worry that jurors might inundate the court with their questions. Even though those judges who have permitted jurors to ask questions have not found that the practice added significant time to a trial, and have found that the questions were reasonable,[10] an elongated trial process remains a concern. Finally, judges, many of whom espouse a traditional view of the juror's role as passive, wonder why it is necessary to alter courtroom practices in any way. They reason that not allowing jurors to ask questions has worked well in the past, so why is there any need to experiment with this new practice now?

There are several reasons to experiment and to allow jurors to ask questions. If jurors are confused during the trial, they are likely to remain in that state unless they are permitted to seek clarification. By asking their questions and having their confusions addressed by the court, jurors will be able to focus on the remainder of the trial and presumably will understand what is happening. Without this opportunity, the main option is to turn to fellow jurors once deliberations have begun; however, fellow jurors may or may not know the answer. If none of the jurors knows the answer, then jurors

---

10. *See* Nicole L. Mott, *The Current Debate on Juror Questions: "To Ask or Not To Ask, That Is the Question,"* 78 CHI.-KENT L. REV. 1099, 1120 (2003) (finding that judges who allowed jurors to ask questions thought their questions were reasonable and did not significantly lengthen the trial process).

may begin to speculate. Such speculation takes place behind the closed door of the jury room and beyond the court's supervision. Another alternative, albeit impermissible and undesirable, is for jurors to engage in self-help. There are instances in which jurors have, on their own, made site visits[11] or consulted reference books, the Internet, and lawyers who are not involved in the case.[12] In light of the alternatives, it seems better for the parties if the jurors have their questions answered by the court; it also seems better for the jurors. Otherwise, the jurors are likely to feel that they are being denied the very tools they need to perform their job as competently as possible.

In most states, the decision whether to permit juror questions is left to the discretion of the trial judge. In a few states, such as Mississippi, juror questions are prohibited by state procedural rules; whereas in a few others, such as Texas, Georgia, and Minnesota, they are prohibited only in criminal cases.[13] In a few states, such as Arizona, Florida,

11. *See, e.g.*, People v. Collins, 813 N.E.2d 285 (Ill. 2004) (reversing and remanding the judgment of conviction in light of the foreperson's visit to the crime scene on the second day of trial, which he had undertaken to better understand " 'where people were on the scene' ") (quoting foreperson).

12. *See, e.g.*, Martin Berg, *Investigator's Main Focus: Probing Juror Misconduct*, L.A. DAILY J., Oct. 26, 1994, at 2 ("The kind of misconduct uncovered [by Public Interest Investigations] has to do with jurors conducting their own investigations, or even philosophical inquiries. 'One juror in a capital case brought in notes from Calvin and Thomas Aquinas. . . .' ") (quoting private investigator Keith Rohman).

13. *See* Mott, *supra* note 10, at 1100.

and Indiana, juror questions are permitted by state procedural rules.[14] In general, though, the practice has not been widely adopted yet; only a few higher courts have had the opportunity to weigh in on whether they find juror questions permissible.[15] Interestingly, the practice of allowing jurors to ask questions, like the practice of permitting jurors to take notes, gained support from judges and lawyers alike when they actually had experience with it in the courtroom.[16]

Jurors' Predeliberation Discussions

An even more experimental practice than permitting jurors to ask questions during the trial is permitting them to engage in discussion of the case prior to their official deliberations. The idea behind this practice is that it is human nature for jurors to want to discuss the trial, which they are required to observe for days, weeks, and sometimes months. Most courts turn a blind eye to the fact that jurors do engage in predeliberation discussions, albeit on an informal and ad hoc basis and contrary to judicial instructions.[17] Those judges who officially per-

14. *See id.*

15. *But see* State v. Costello, 646 N.W.2d 204 (Minn. 2002) (holding that juror questions threaten the juror's proper role in the adversarial system).

16. *See* Larry Heurer & Steven Penrod, *Increasing Juror Participation in Trials Through Note Taking and Question Asking*, 79 JUDICATURE 256, 259, 261 (1996).

17. *See* Elizabeth F. Loftus & Douglas Leber, *Do Jurors Talk?*, TRIAL, Jan. 1986, at 59 (estimating that 10 to 11% of jurors discuss the trial with family, friends, and other jurors before they begin deliberations).

mit predeliberation discussion have done so in part because they believe it is a way for jurors to begin to process, organize, and retain the wealth of information that is presented to them during the trial, and in part because it is a way to provide guidelines for discussions that are likely to take place anyway, judicial admonitions notwithstanding.

At least one state, Arizona, allows jurors to engage in predeliberation discussions in civil trials.[18] Judges in Arizona provide jurors with some guidelines for these discussions. For example, judges instruct jurors that they only can engage in predeliberation discussions when they are in the jury room and when all jurors are present. They also remind jurors that it is their responsibility to keep an open mind and that these preliminary discussions should not lead them to take a position for one side or the other. These early discussions are mainly to answer questions, share impressions, and make note of points that they would like to take up during the official deliberations.

Several researchers sought to study the efficacy of Arizona's jury reforms, including predeliberation discussions. They secured the permission of the Arizona judiciary and recorded, transcribed, and analyzed several juries' predeliberation discussions, as well as their actual deliberations.[19] Among their

18. *See* ARIZ. R. 39(f) (Admonition to Jurors; Juror Discussions).

19. There is a federal statute, 18 U.S.C. § 1508, that prohibits the recording or filming of any jury deliberations in federal courts. Most states have similar statutes. On occasion, however,

findings was that jurors did not always adhere to all of the judge's admonitions.[20] For example, jurors did not always wait until all jurors were present before engaging in predeliberation discussions.[21] Such empirical research will help the Arizona judiciary to fine-tune this innovative jury practice.

Without question, Arizona is in the vanguard of jury reform, and most other states are unwilling to introduce such new practices. With predeliberation discussions, judges generally worry that jurors will form a point of view too early in the proceedings, perhaps even before both sides have presented their case. Even though judges typically discuss a case with their law clerks throughout the trial, they worry that when jurors discuss a case at such an early stage in the proceedings, they may form a point of view and be unwilling to shift even as new exhibits or testimony should move them in another direction. They also worry that some jurors—name-

state judges, with the consent of the parties, lawyers, and jurors, have permitted jury deliberations to be filmed. *See, e.g., Frontline: Inside the Jury Room* (WGBH broadcast, Apr. 8, 1986) (filming a Wisconsin jury deliberating about the felony charge against Leroy Reed); *CBS Reports: Enter the Jury Room* (CBS broadcast, Apr. 16, 1997) (filming the deliberations of several Arizona juries); *In the Jury Room* (ABC broadcast, Aug. 10 & 11, 2004) (filming the trial and jury deliberations in an Ohio State court capital case).

20. *See, e.g.,* Hannaford et al., *supra* note 42 (Ch. 3), at 376, 379 (finding that jurors engaged in a relatively high level of informal discussion with family, friends, or other jurors in spite of the judge's admonition to refrain from discussion with others).

21. *See id.* at 376 (finding that juries permitted to engage in preverdict deliberations did so without always waiting for all jurors to be present).

ly the more dominant ones—might have too great an influence on other jurors, particularly when they are at a formative stage in their thinking about the case. Finally, judges also worry that jurors who engage in predeliberation discussions might believe that they already know each other's views, and therefore, they fail to listen to each other during the actual deliberations.

Given judges' concerns about the practice, the most likely impetus for change will be the Arizona judges' actual experience with jurors' predeliberation discussions. If the Arizona experiment shows that jurors can discuss a case without drawing conclusions and that it helps them to understand and absorb the material presented at trial, then other states are likely to follow Arizona's lead.

CHAPTER 7

JUDICIAL CONTROL OVER JURORS DURING TRIAL

As discussed in the previous chapter, judges and lawyers are reluctant to transform passive jurors into active jurors during trial. One reason that judges may resist this transformation is that the more active and self-reliant jurors are during trial, the less control judges will have over them and the trial proceedings. Jurors typically begin their jury experience by viewing the judge with great deference. Jurors are laypersons, and look up to the judge, who is an authority figure, robed in black, seated on high, with gavel in hand; clearly, the judge is experienced and in control of the proceedings. The less information jurors are given about the trial, and the more bewildering the experience is for them, the more likely they are to continue to take their cues from the judge. However, the more information and tools jurors are given to understand the proceedings, the less they are going to have to rely wholly upon the judge and the more they are going to be able to think for themselves.

In spite of this tension, judges still have many ways, some subtle and some more obvious, of exercising control over jurors during the trial. One source of judicial power is simply their position as a figure of authority; a second source is the judge's instructions to the jury; and a third source is the judge's role as gatekeeper, which allows the judge to decide which evidence goes to the jury and which is withheld from it.

A Judge's Position of Authority

The judge, by virtue of his or her position of authority, is typically held in high esteem by jurors.[1] When prospective jurors enter the courtroom as part of a venire, they have little idea what to expect. The judge welcomes them, and to the extent they receive any explanation as to how jury selection will proceed, the judge provides it. The voir dire, which the judge either conducts or supervises,[2] introduces jurors to the role of the judge, which is that of a neutral arbiter, responsible for providing the parties with an impartial jury and a fair trial.

The judge also sets the tone in the courtroom. A good judge will treat the jury with respect, and good lawyers will follow suit. In some courtrooms, the judge (and everyone else in the courtroom) will rise whenever the jury enters and exits the courtroom, as a sign of respect for the jury. A judge who fosters respect for the jury is also likely to earn the respect of the jury.

1. *But see* D. GRAHAM BURNETT, A TRIAL BY JURY (2001) (describing a case in which the trial judge was viewed by jurors as harsh and unreasonable, and therefore, was not a source of information to which the jurors willingly turned).

2. *See supra* text accompanying notes 53–56 (Ch. 5) (describing who should conduct the voir dire).

The judge also derives some of his or her authority by serving as a source of information for and guidance to the jurors. Once a jury is empanelled, the judge begins by giving jurors some background about the case and the nature of the jurors' task. After this introduction, jurors become accustomed to turning to the judge for explanations of what is happening and what is expected of them. After all, jurors are usually laypersons with little familiarity with the law (other than what they glean from movies, television, and newspapers). The judge is fully versed in the law, and indeed, is charged with presenting it to the jurors in as neutral a manner as possible. Although lawyers will present their version of the case and the law to the jurors, the jurors quickly recognize that lawyers are advocates; the judge, as well as the jury, occupies a position of neutrality in the courtroom. Thus, it is from the judge that the jurors will acquire much of the information they need to perform their own role.

Jurors also will look to the judge as a model for how they should perform their own role. A judge is a neutral arbiter in the courtroom, and the jurors are also supposed to be neutral decision-makers. A judge is supposed to withhold judgment until the end of a case, and jurors, too, learn to aspire to this goal. The jurors, then, hold the judge in high regard, not just by virtue of his or her position, but also for what the judge can teach jurors about their own role.

Indeed, Alexis de Tocqueville, writing almost 170 years ago about the American jury system, explained that jury service in a civil trial was likely to teach jurors how to be good citizens because they would emulate the judge, and in so doing, they would learn how to think judiciously.[3] Tocqueville discerned that the jury's most important function was not as a judicial institution, but rather as a "political institution."[4] The jury was a political institution in that it provided citizens with an opportunity to participate in their own self-governance. In this sense, then, it served as a "free school,"[5] teaching jurors about democracy; and in this free school, the judge was the teacher. Juries teach men[6]

> equity in practice. Each man, when judging his neighbor, thinks that he may be judged himself.
>
> . . . .
>
> Juries teach each individual not to shirk responsibility for his own acts, and without that manly characteristic no political virtue is possible.
>
> Juries invest each citizen with a sort of magisterial office; they make all men feel that they have duties toward society and that they take a share in its government.[7]

3. *See* Tocqueville, *supra* note 7 (Ch. 2), at 274.

4. *Id.* at 272.

5. *Id.* at 275.

6. And indeed, when Tocqueville wrote *Democracy in America*, it was only men who could serve as jurors in federal and state courts. *See* Marder, *supra* note 15 (Ch. 3), at 889 n.43 (providing a brief history of women's exclusion from jury duty).

7. Tocqueville, *supra* note 7 (Ch. 2), at 274.

For Tocqueville, the civil jury experience provided greater opportunities for the judge to influence jurors than the criminal jury experience.[8] Tocqueville surmised that criminal matters might appear more straightforward to jurors, whereas, in civil matters, they might have greater need for the expertise of the judge. Also, in criminal matters, the jurors might view the judge as another arm of government, whereas their role was to serve as a buffer between the government and the criminal defendant. In civil matters, however, they faced no such conflict. Therefore, Tocqueville reasoned, jurors were more likely to take their cue from the judge in a civil case. The effect would be far-reaching because, as Tocqueville observed, most people did not come into contact with the criminal justice system in their everyday lives and so what they learned in the courtroom in a criminal case was less likely to be applicable to their lives after they had completed their jury service. In contrast, civil matters often involved disputes that arose in ordinary business. What jurors learned from civil cases, they could take with them when they resumed their private lives after jury service. Thus, if they learned from the judge how to think about a business dispute in a judicious manner, they could take this reasoning and apply it to their daily business pursuits.

One reason Tocqueville might have portrayed the judge as a teacher who could exert great influence over jurors, particularly in civil cases, was because he was trying to persuade French judges to experi-

8. *Id.* at 275.

ment with juries and wanted to convince them that
rather than viewing juries as a threat to their power
they should view juries as a way to extend the reach
of their power.[9] Even though Tocqueville described
the jury as a democratizing institution that would
enable those who served as jurors to be better
citizens, the message that he conveyed to French
judges was that jurors, particularly in civil cases,
would be susceptible to the lessons instilled by
judges. Thus, the institution of the jury would enable judges to shape men's minds, to spread the
benefits of judicious thinking beyond the walls of
the courthouse, and even to enhance judges' position in society. Although Tocqueville undoubtedly
overstated the extent to which judges influence
jurors, particularly in civil cases, his point that they
can influence jurors still holds true today.

Indeed, empirical studies[10] suggest that jurors
continue to take their cues from judges in ways so
subtle that judges and jurors might be unaware of
them. According to one early study, jurors look to
judges for guidance because they are uncertain how
to perform their own role.[11] Even today, jurors look
to the judge because of anxiety about what they are

9. *Id.* at 276.

10. *See, e.g.,* Note, *The Appearance of Justice: Judges' Verbal
and Nonverbal Behavior in Criminal Jury Trials*, 38 STAN. L. REV.
89 (1985) [hereinafter *The Appearance of Justice*]; Note, *Judges'
Nonverbal Behavior in Jury Trials: A Threat to Judicial Impartiality*, 61 VA. L. REV. 1266, 1278 (1975) [hereinafter *Judges'
Nonverbal Behavior in Jury Trials*].

11. *See Judges' Nonverbal Behavior in Jury Trials, supra*
note 10, at 1278.

expected to do.[12] According to another study, jurors are influenced not only by what a judge says, but also by the way in which he or she says it.[13] Judges may inadvertently convey their expectations for a trial outcome to jurors through subtle, nonverbal cues, such as facial expressions or tone of voice.[14] Such nonverbal communication is difficult to capture and preserve for the record, making review by appellate judges, who would usually serve as a check on how a trial judge has conducted a trial, less effective.[15]

A Judge's Instructions to the Jury

Another source of judicial control over jurors during trial is the instructions that a judge provides. Although there are many shortcomings with judicial instructions—from a judge's delivery of instructions typically at the end of trial to a judge's use of legal jargon in crafting the instructions—they nonetheless have a constraining effect on jurors and are a way in which a judge exercises some control over the jury both during trial and deliberations.

12. *See, e.g.,* Robert J. Hirsh et al., *Attorney Voir Dire and Arizona's Jury Reform Package,* ARIZ. ATT'Y, Apr. 1996, at 24, 32 ("Jurors very quickly pick up on judges' expectations and mannerisms.... While it is seldom the intention of judges to reveal these, expectations of the court for the jurors in the courtrooms are usually quite evident, especially to those anxious jurors.").

13. *See The Appearance of Justice, supra* note 10, at 89.

14. *Id.* at 100.

15. *Id.* ("Appellate courts recognize that the appearance of judicial bias or unfairness at the trial can be manifested by trial judges in explicit and subtle verbal and 'nonverbal' ways that never show up on the 'dry' appellate record.").

After a jury is selected, the jurors rise and take an oath. In this oath, they swear to follow the law as the judge instructs them on it. A typical juror's oath is as follows: "You and each of you, do solemnly swear that you will well and truly try the cause now pending before this Court, and a true verdict render therein, according to the evidence and the instructions of the Court, so help you God?"[16] Although oaths may not be viewed with as much dread as they once were when it was assumed that dire consequences would befall the man who broke his oath, an oath is still a serious matter today. Jurors take an oath declaring that they will follow the law as the judge gives it to them. Thus, beginning with the oath, jurors are on notice that the instructions the judge gives them on the law are meant to be followed, not questioned.[17]

Through judicial instructions, the judge informs jurors of the law that they are to apply to the facts as they find them. One source of the jury's power is its fact-finding; one source of the judge's power is his or her instructions on the law. Typically, the judge instructs the jury on the law after both parties have completed their closing arguments but before the jury retires to the jury room for deliberations. One limitation with this timing is that some of the instructions would have been useful for jurors to know during the trial. For example, an instruction on how to evaluate the testimony of a

16. CALIFORNIA SUPERIOR COURT CRIMINAL TRIAL JUDGES' DESKBOOK 356 (Ronald M. George ed., 1988 ed.).

17. *But see* Marder, *supra* note 15 (Ch. 3), at 926–34 (describing the benefits of nullification in rare instances).

law enforcement officer—in which jurors are instructed that a law enforcement officer's testimony
is to be given no more or less weight than the
testimony of any other witness[18]—would be useful
for jurors to have before they hear such testimony.
Therefore, some judges have experimented with giving instructions as the trial proceeds, on a "need-to-
know" basis, as well as at the end of the trial.[19]

Another limitation with the traditional timing of
jury instructions is that it means that jurors must
listen to the judge read instructions for hours at a
time. As every student knows, it is difficult to
absorb a lengthy lecture, particularly if one cannot
take notes or ask questions. Therefore, some judges
not only read the instructions to jurors, but also
give them individual written copies of the instructions so that they can listen to the instructions as
well as follow along as the instructions are read;[20]
jurors also can take the written instructions into
the jury room and refer back to them when necessary. The next step in instructions, as judges be-

18. *See, e.g.*, 1 LEONARD B. SAND ET AL., MODERN FEDERAL JURY
INSTRUCTIONS: CRIMINAL 7–16 (2004) (Law Enforcement Witness).

19. *See, e.g.,* B. Michael Dann & George Logan III, *Jury
Reform: The Arizona Experience*, 79 JUDICATURE 280, 280 (1996)
(describing structural changes that should be adopted by Arizona
courts, such as giving trial judges discretion about the timing of
judicial instructions).

20. Judges deliver instructions orally and give jurors written
copies of the instructions to follow because "material is better
remembered when it is presented in several different forms than
in a single form. Having the jurors both listen to and read the
instructions should capitalize on this effect." JURY TRIAL INNOVA-
TIONS, *supra* note 22 (Ch. 5), at 19.

come more willing to make use of technology, will be to allow jurors to take into the jury room an audiotape or videotape of the judge reading the instructions so that the jurors can replay parts as the need arises during their deliberations and have the benefit of the judge's phrasing and intonation as they try to parse the meaning of the instructions.

Of course, one reason that parsing is necessary is because jury instructions, in spite of their name, are written more for lawyers and appellate judges than for jurors. The incomprehensibility of jury instructions has long been a subject of study and debate.[21] The instructions often make use of legal terms and phrases that few laypersons know. The grammatical constructions are often awkward, making sentences hard for jurors to follow.[22] The organization of the instructions is difficult to discern. One would have to be familiar with case law, which most jurors are not, to understand why the instructions use the words, phrases, and structure that they do. Finally, many trial judges rely on *pattern instructions*—the

21. *See generally* AMIRAM ELWORK ET AL., MAKING JURY INSTRUCTIONS UNDERSTANDABLE (1982) (providing guidelines for improving jury instructions); Bruce Sales et al., *Improving Comprehension for Jury Instructions*, *in* 1 PERSPECTIVES IN LAW & PSYCHOLOGY: THE CRIMINAL JUSTICE SYSTEM 23 (B. Sales ed., 1977) (explaining that jury instructions' comprehensibility can be improved through attention to vocabulary, grammatical construction, and organization).

22. *See, e.g.,* Robert P. Charrow & Veda R. Charrow, *Making Legal Language Understandable: A Psycholinguistic Study of Jury Instructions*, 79 COLUM. L. REV. 1306 (1979) (finding that jury instructions are made difficult by awkward grammatical constructions).

basic, boiler-plate instructions that judges can simply use without making many changes—because they have been approved by appellate judges over time.[23] Although pattern instructions ensure a certain consistency in the instructions, they also lead trial judges to be wary about altering the instructions, even when jurors ask for clarification. Trial judges worry that any extemporaneous remarks they make or examples they give to assist jurors might lead to reversal on appeal.[24]

Jury instructions often fall short of their basic goals. They are the chief means by which the judge educates jurors about the law, their role throughout the trial, and during deliberations. Although jurors often fail to understand the instructions—a failure that has been well documented in myriad studies—judges have been slow to acknowledge this failure and rewrite the instructions. For example, California judges initially resisted a recent effort to rewrite pattern instructions into "plain English" in spite of grass-roots support for such an effort.[25] What these

23.   For an example of a book of pattern jury instructions, see ILLINOIS PATTERN JURY INSTRUCTIONS, CIVIL (IPI)(2000).

24.   At one conference, Federal District Court Judge Stanley Sporkin, when asked why he did not break with past practice in letting jurors take notes or in improving jury instructions, looked over to then Chief Judge Abner Mikva of the United States Court of Appeals for the District of Columbia, and explained: " '[Chief Judge Mikva] would overturn me.' " Fred H. Cate & Newton N. Minow, *Communicating with Juries*, 68 INDIANA L.J. 1101, 1111 (1993).

25.   *See, e.g.*, Mike Kataoka, *Eschewing Obfuscation: The Judicial Council Strives for Plain English With Its New Jury Instructions*, CAL. LAW., Dec. 2000, at 53.

and other judges fail to consider about current instructions is that they interfere with jurors' understanding of the law, as well as with judges' opportunity to influence jurors.

The cases in which jury instructions play the most important role are those in which the death penalty is at issue and it is the jury's task to recommend or decide the sentence.[26] In those cases, it is critical that jurors understand the law as the judge instructs them on it. The sources of misunderstanding have been numerous and well-documented by social scientists, psychologists, and legal scholars.[27] Some of the misunderstandings arise from a layperson's lack of familiarity with terms, such as "aggravating circumstances" and "mitigating evidence," that have a particular meaning when they are used in state statutes pertaining to the death penalty. Another misunderstanding arises from whether terms are to be understood literally or in their ordinary, everyday meaning. For example, how should jurors interpret "life imprisonment"? Does it mean that a defendant sentenced to such a term would actually spend his entire life in jail ("literal meaning"), or does it mean that he would be released in a few years, as appeared to be the common practice in many states and reported in the press ("ordinary, everyday meaning")?

26. For a list of states in which the jury decides (sometimes in conjunction with the judge) whether to impose a life or death sentence, see Marder, *supra* note 15 (Ch. 3), at 891 n.62.

27. *See, e.g.,* Theodore Eisenberg & Martin T. Wells, *Deadly Confusion: Juror Instructions in Capital Cases*, 79 CORNELL L. REV. 1 (1993).

Juror misunderstandings of instructions in death penalty cases are further exacerbated when knowledge is deliberately withheld from the jury. For example, in *Simmons v. South Carolina*,[28] the prosecutor argued that the defendant would be a "future danger" to society if not sentenced to death. However, the defendant was not permitted to respond that he could not be a "future danger" to society because he was in prison where he would remain for the rest of his life as, under a South Carolina statute, he was ineligible for parole. The defense, after reviewing the results of a public opinion survey, was concerned that the jurors, like those who had been polled, believed that "life imprisonment" did not actually mean imprisonment for life, but only for a limited amount of time, after which the defendant would be released.[29] Indeed, the jury in *Simmons* sent a note to the judge asking whether " 'imposition of a life sentence carr[ies] with it the possibility of parole.' "[30] The judge responded by instructing the jury not to consider parole or the parole eligibility of the defendant. Twenty-five minutes later, the jury returned with a sentence of death.[31]

The U.S. Supreme Court reversed the judgment in *Simmons*, reasoning that the defendant had a right under the Due Process Clause of the Fourteenth Amendment to rebut the prosecutor's argument about future dangerousness and to correct the "grievous misperception" that life imprisonment

28. 512 U.S. 154 (1994).
29. *Id.* at 159.
30. *Id.* at 160.
31. *Id.*

would not mean imprisonment for life in this case.[32] Without such clarification, the jury was left to "speculate" about the meaning of life imprisonment in this case and was "denied a straight answer," even after it had asked for one.[33] The South Carolina trial judge had denied the defendant his due process right to challenge the prosecutor's argument and had deprived the jury of complete information about defendant's parole ineligiblity.

A Judge as Gatekeeper

A third way in which the judge maintains control over the jury at trial is as gatekeeper. The judge performs this function insofar as he or she decides which evidence will be presented to the jury and which will be kept from it. Traditionally, judges performed this function in as minimally intrusive a fashion as possible. As long as the evidence was relevant, and unless it met one of the exceptions, such as being highly prejudicial, the judge's tendency was to allow it in and to leave it to the jury to decide how much weight to give it. Recently, however, the Supreme Court expanded the judge's role as gatekeeper. In matters involving scientific evidence, the Supreme Court has instructed trial judges to decide in the first instance how reliable the scientific studies are before allowing experts to testify to them at trial.[34] This expansion of the judge's role as

32. *Id.* at 165.

33. *Id.* at 171.

34. *See* Daubert v. Merrell Dow Pharmaceuticals, 509 U.S. 579 (1993).

gatekeeper reflects a growing distrust of juries to decide such matters as part of their fact-finding role. Yet, in one area in which juries could use the assistance of judges and their gatekeeping function—when assessing the reliability of eyewitness testimony—appellate judges have *not* required trial judges to serve as gatekeepers.

Eyewitness Testimony

Eyewitness testimony is one of the least reliable and yet one of the most trusted forms of testimony that jurors confront at trial. An eyewitness is someone who says: "I was there, and this is what I saw." Whether in civil or criminal matters, eyewitness testimony is very persuasive. It is human nature to believe that we can trust what we have seen and that we can trust what others say that they have seen. This is a strongly held, common-sense belief that is difficult to dislodge.

In spite of this common-sense view that eyewitness testimony is reliable and should be believed, numerous empirical studies have demonstrated the unreliability of eyewitness testimony.[35] There are many factors that interfere with the accuracy of eyewitness testimony, such as the conditions under which the eyewitness observed the incident or

---

35. *See, e.g.,* ELIZABETH F. LOFTUS, EYEWITNESS TESTIMONY (1979); John C. Brigham & Robert K. Bothwell, *The Ability of Prospective Jurors to Estimate the Accuracy of Eyewitness Identifications,* 7 LAW & HUM. BEHAV. 19 (1987); Frederic D. Woocher, Note, *Did Your Eyes Deceive You? Expert Psychological Testimony on the Unreliability of Eyewitness Identification,* 29 STAN. L. REV. 969 (1977).

crime:[36] How ordinary was the situation? How far away was the eyewitness? How long was the period of observation? What was the lighting like? Was the eyewitness in danger? What was the gender, race, or ethnicity of the person being observed and of the observer?

The answers to these and other questions can affect how reliable the eyewitness testimony is. For example, if the eyewitness is in danger, the testimony is less likely to be reliable because the eyewitness is more likely to focus on how to escape from danger than to pay attention to details needed for future identification.[37] If conditions for observation are poor (the eyewitness is far away; it is dark; the incident lasted only a few, fleeting seconds), then the testimony is also likely to be unreliable. Finally, stereotypes are likely to be a factor. According to one study in which participants were shown an illustration and then asked to recall it, the African-American man pictured in a subway car was more likely to be seen as the person holding the razor rather than the white man standing next to him who actually held the razor.[38] Other studies also have shown that cross-racial identification is more difficult for eyewitnesses to make accurately than identification of members of one's own race.[39]

36. *See* Robert Buckhout, *Eyewitness Testimony*, Sci. Am., Dec. 1974, at 23, 24–25.

37. *Id.* at 25.

38. *See id.* at 26 (describing this "classic study," conducted by Gordon W. Allport of Harvard).

39. *See id.*

In spite of these difficulties, eyewitness testimony is exceedingly persuasive.[40] When an eyewitness says "I saw that person commit the crime," that is difficult testimony to call into question, particularly if the eyewitness speaks with confidence.[41] Even if other evidence undercuts the eyewitness testimony, the eyewitness testimony is still believed.[42] For example, if the eyewitness identifies the defendant as the perpetrator, even though the perpetrator was originally said to be six feet tall and the defendant is five feet six inches tall and has an alibi that he was at work at the time to which nine of his co-workers can attest, the eyewitness is still going to be believed.[43] Not surprisingly, there are numerous

40. *See, e.g.,* Brigham & Bothwell, *supra* note 35, at 27 (noting that jurors find eyewitness evidence extremely persuasive).

41. *See* ELIZABETH LOFTUS & JAMES DOYLE, EYEWITNESS TESTIMONY, § 1.02, at 25 (1987) ("The confidence of the eyewitness was a crucial determinant of believability. The jurors tended to believe those witnesses who were highly confident more than they believed those who were not.").

42. *See* LOFTUS, *supra* note 35, at 9 ("Jurors have been known to accept eyewitness testimony pointing to guilt even when it is *far* outweighed by evidence of innocence.") (emphasis in original); Woocher, *supra* note 35, at 970 ("For the layperson, visual identification of the defendant by the victim or witness often provides the most persuasive evidence, which cannot be overcome by contrary evidence supporting the accused.").

43. *See* KASSIN & WRIGHTSMAN, *supra* note 5 (Ch. 6), at 79 (describing the case involving Lennell Geter, convicted and sentenced to life imprisonment based on eyewitness testimony and no physical evidence; Geter was eventually released but only after he had spent more than a year in prison.).

examples of wrongful convictions based on eyewitness testimony.[44]

In spite of the cases of erroneous eyewitness identification and the studies documenting the many factors that lead eyewitness testimony to be unreliable, courts have been loath to step in and advise juries about these possible sources of error. This is an area that is supposed to rely on common sense and because jurors, as laypersons, are supposed to bring their common-sense judgment to the decision-making process, this is one area where courts have been reluctant to interfere.

When courts do consider possible ways to suggest to juries that eyewitness testimony can be unreliable, the least intrusive way is through a cautionary instruction. However, there are several reasons why such an instruction is not particularly effective. First, such an instruction tends to be general and vague, and takes the form of: "You should decide how much weight to give the eyewitness testimony you have heard." Second, such an instruction is given in the context of myriad other instructions, so that the jury may not give it the attention that it deserves. Third, the common-sense notion that we can believe what we see is so strong that even a cautionary instruction urging jurors to take a close look at the eyewitness testimony does little to dislodge that strongly held belief.

44. As the Supreme Court once observed: "The vagaries of eyewitness identification are well-known; the annals of criminal law are rife with instances of mistaken identification." United States v. Wade, 388 U.S. 218, 228 (1967). For numerous examples of mistaken identification, see Marder, *supra* note 95 (Ch. 5), at 1041, 1072 n.123.

In cases in which there is eyewitness testimony, some judges have permitted experts to testify about memory, perception, and eyewitness testimony. Such testimony can encourage jurors to take a closer look at eyewitness testimony and to consider whether there were factors present that might make it more or less reliable. The difficulty with hiring an expert to highlight the unreliability of eyewitness testimony, however, is that the other side is likely to hire its own expert to highlight the reliability of eyewitness testimony. The jury is then left with dueling experts. One common response, in the face of "a battle of the experts," is simply to ignore both experts.

A more radical response, which has been mentioned but not adopted, is to allow eyewitness testimony only when there is other corroborating evidence.[45] The difficulty with this approach is that there are many situations in which there is no corroborating evidence. Therefore, if this were a requirement, there would be many crimes that could not be prosecuted even though there had been an eyewitness. This result would seriously undermine criminal prosecutions, and therefore, seems unlikely to be adopted.

Eyewitness testimony presents judges with a gatekeeping conundrum: They are not supposed to act as gatekeepers with respect to eyewitness testimony because it relies on the common-sense notion that we can trust what we see and jurors do not need assistance when it comes to common sense; yet,

45. *See* KASSIN & WRIGHTSMAN, *supra* note 5 (Ch. 6), at 83.

empirical studies suggest that the common-sense notion is wrong and that the testimony can be unreliable in highly counterintuitive ways. This is an area that cries out for the judge to serve as gatekeeper, and yet, because it involves common sense, it is an area that is usually devoid of judicial intervention. Thus, eyewitness testimony, which has been the subject of much empirical study, is left to the jury to assess in spite of evidence of common misunderstandings and mistakes. In contrast, scientific evidence, which is not as widely documented as a source of jury error, has become an area in which judges have been instructed to serve as gatekeepers.

Scientific Evidence

With the Supreme Court opinion in *Daubert v. Merrell Dow Pharmaceuticals*,[46] followed by two other Supreme Court opinions,[47] trial judges now serve as gatekeepers for scientific evidence, or in the lament of one commentator, "as gate[s] that start[] in the closed position."[48] They must first decide whether an expert's testimony is relevant and has a reliable foundation in the scientific community before it can be presented to the jury. By

46. 509 U.S. 579 (1993).

47. *See* General Electric Co. v. Joiner, 522 U.S. 136 (1997); Kumho Tire Co. v. Carmichael, 526 U.S. 137 (1999).

48. Frank Tuerkheimer, *The* Daubert *Case and Its Aftermath: A Shot-Gun Wedding of Technology and Law in the Supreme Court*, 51 SYRACUSE L. REV. 803, 828 (2001) ("Indeed, the term 'gatekeeper,' so freely used in *Daubert* for the envisaged trial court role does not quite fit; just 'gate' might be a better description of the district court function portended by the three Supreme Court cases.").

giving the judge this control, the Supreme Court has revealed a certain distrust of experts and juries, and, at the same time, has expanded the role of the judge in the courtroom.

The judge is not entirely new to this role as gatekeeper with respect to scientific evidence. Under the earlier standard for federal courts set forth in *Frye v. United States*,[49] the judge performed this role, albeit in a more general, less searching, manner. In *Frye*, a 1923 case that predated the *Federal Rules of Evidence* by about fifty years, the defendant wanted to introduce evidence of a systolic blood pressure deception test, a precursor to the polygraph test. The trial judge did not allow the expert who administered the test to be introduced to the jury nor the test itself to be demonstrated to the jury.[50] The Court of Appeals for the District of Columbia affirmed the exclusion of this evidence, reasoning that the systolic blood pressure deception test had not yet gained "general acceptance" among "physiological and psychological authorities as would justify the courts in admitting expert testimony."[51]

Frye established that for an expert to testify on scientific evidence, his view had to be one for which there was general acceptance by the scientific community of which he was a member. Under *Frye*, then, a trial judge had to decide that the expert was qualified and that his method was generally accept-

49.   293 F. 1013 (D.C. Cir. 1923).

50.   *Id.* at 1014.

51.   *Id.*

ed in his field. However, the *Frye* test was not
without its difficulties.[52] The requirement that the
method have "general acceptance" in the scientific
community meant that scientific tests which had
some acceptance, but not general acceptance, would
not be admitted. In addition, it was hard to define
exactly what constituted the scientific community.
However, one advantage of the *Frye* test was that
the judge did not have to make any determination
about the conclusions the expert had reached. The
trial judge was able to take a "hands-off" approach
toward expert evidence, leaving it to the scientific
community to determine the reliability of the test
and leaving it to the jury, as trier of fact, to decide
what weight to give the expert's testimony.

In *Daubert*,[53] the Supreme Court revisited the
Frye standard. *Daubert* involved a suit brought by
two minor children, along with their parents, who
claimed that the drug Bendectin, manufactured by
defendant Merrell Dow and taken by the women
during their pregnancies, had caused the children's
birth defects.[54] Published studies had failed to find
such a causal connection. However, plaintiffs wanted to introduce several experts whose own research

52. *Frye* had been the subject of numerous articles by academics, in which they had debated its limitations and asked
whether its utility had long since passed. The Court in *Daubert*
made note of this extensive academic commentary on *Frye* as
well as the way in which courts were divided on the subject. *See
Daubert*, 509 U.S. at 587 nn.4 & 5.

53. *Id.* at 579.

54. Plaintiffs filed suit in California state court, but defendant removed the case to federal court based on diversity jurisdiction. *See* 28 U.S.C. § 1332.

had shown that Bendectin could cause birth defects in humans. The trial judge ruled plaintiffs' evidence inadmissible in part because it was a reanalysis of existing data and in part because it had not been published or subject to peer review.[55] The trial judge granted summary judgment for defendant, and plaintiffs appealed. The Ninth Circuit, in a brief opinion by Judge Kozinski, affirmed, reasoning that the evidence did not meet the *Frye* standard of being generally accepted within the scientific community;[56] the Supreme Court vacated the judgment and remanded the case.[57]

The *Daubert* Court, after noting that the *Frye* test was superseded by the adoption of the *Federal Rules of Evidence*,[58] announced a new standard for trial judges to use in deciding whether to admit expert testimony on scientific matters. According to *Daubert*, the trial judge must decide whether the scientific evidence is relevant, and if so, whether it is reliable.[59] Although the opinion tried to craft a flexible test, and to move away from what it viewed as the "rigid[ity]" of *Frye*,[60] and toward the "flexib[ility]" envisaged by *Federal Rule of Evidence* 702,[61] in fact, the test ends up being far more restrictive as to the admission of this evidence and

55. *Daubert*, 509 U.S. at 583.

56. *Id.* at 584.

57. *Id.* at 598.

58. *Id.* at 587.

59. *Id.* at 589.

60. *Id.* at 588.

61. 509 U.S. at 594.

puts the trial judge in the awkward position of having to play "scientist." This, in turn, diminishes the jury's role.

The *Daubert* opinion sets forth several factors that trial judges should look to in deciding whether to admit expert testimony on scientific matters. These factors include whether the theory has been tested; whether it has been subjected to peer review and publication; what the relevant error rate is; and whether the theory is generally accepted.[62] Justice Blackmun, writing for the Court in *Daubert*, described the trial judge as performing "a gatekeeping role" which will "on occasion ... prevent the jury from learning of authentic insights and innovations."[63] Chief Justice Rehnquist, in an opinion in which he concurred in part and dissented in part, agreed with the Court that the *Frye* rule was superseded by the *Federal Rules of Evidence*, but disagreed that the Court should have proceeded to address, in general and abstract terms, the factors that lower courts should consider in determining the admissibility of expert testimony.[64] In his view, because this was "dicta," the Court should have refrained from such general discussion. Furthermore, he feared that the Court's expanded gatekeeping role for trial judges was one that would require them to become "amateur scientists."[65] Judge Kozinski expressed similar reservations when

62. *Id.* at 593–94.
63. *Id.* at 597.
64. *Id.* at 598–99.
65. *Id.* at 600–01.

Daubert returned to the Ninth Circuit. He described the difficulty that federal judges now face:

> As we read the Supreme Court's teaching in *Daubert*, therefore, though we are largely untrained in science and certainly no match for any of the witnesses whose testimony we are reviewing, it is our responsibility to determine whether those experts' proposed testimony amounts to 'scientific knowledge,' constitutes 'good science,' and was 'derived by the scientific method.'[66]

The reach of *Daubert* was extended by two subsequent Supreme Court opinions. *General Electric Co. v. Joiner*[67] was brought by Robert Joiner, an electrical worker, who in the course of his work was exposed to PCBs, a substance banned by Congress as a hazardous material. When Joiner developed cancer, he sued his employer, General Electric, on the theory that it was caused by the PCBs. The employer moved for summary judgment on the ground that Joiner would be unable to show a causal link between cancer and PCBs. Joiner's experts thought the cancer was more likely than not caused by the PCBs and relied on several studies, some based on laboratory testing and some based on epidemiological studies. The district court found that the studies provided an insufficient basis and granted summary judgment; the Eleventh Circuit reversed on the ground that there should be a different standard if the exclusion of the evidence

66. Daubert v. Merrell Dow Pharmaceuticals, 43 F.3d 1311, 1316 (9th Cir. 1995).

67. 522 U.S. 136 (1997).

would result in the dismissal of the case. The Supreme Court reversed, holding that the appellate court's standard of review should have been the deferential standard of abuse of discretion. *Daubert* gives the trial judge much control and *Joiner* limits the scrutiny of the appellate judge. *Joiner* also seems to require the trial judge to substitute his judgment for that of the experts: Joiner's experts thought that there was a link between the PCBs and the cancer, the district court judge did not.

Whereas *Frye* was limited to expert testimony on scientific matters, with *Kumho Tire Co. v. Carmichael*,[68] the Court expanded *Daubert* so that it now governs expert testimony on technical and other specialized knowledge as well. In *Kumho Tire Co.*, Patrick Carmichael and others were injured in a car crash as a result of a tire blow-out. The Carmichaels sued the tire's manufacturer and distributor; they sought to establish that defendants were at fault by introducing expert testimony from a former Michelin tire employee. The defendants moved for summary judgment, which was granted by the trial court on the grounds that such expert testimony did not satisfy the four factors of *Daubert*, and therefore, was unreliable. Upon reconsideration, the district court agreed with plaintiffs that the *Daubert* factors were to be applied flexibly, but found that the expert's methodology failed to meet the reliability required by *Daubert* and affirmed its earlier order.[69] The Eleventh Circuit reviewed the district

68. 526 U.S. 137 (1999).

69. *Id.* at 146.

court's ruling and reversed on the theory that *Daubert* was applicable to scientific, not technical, expert testimony,[70] a theory with which the Supreme Court disagreed, and therefore, reversed the Eleventh Circuit.[71]

In *Kumho Tire*, the Court, in an opinion authored by Justice Breyer, held that *Daubert*, flexibly applied, should extend to technical and other specialized knowledge. This approach, the Court believed, was consistent with *Federal Rule of Evidence* 702, which did not distinguish among these different types of expert testimony.[72] In addition, the Court reasoned that it would be "difficult, if not impossible," for trial judges to distinguish between scientific expert testimony on the one hand and technical or other specialized expert testimony on the other hand.[73] For example, technical knowledge, such as in engineering, has a scientific basis. To have one set of factors applicable to scientific expert testimony and another applicable to technical or other specialized expert testimony appeared unworkable. The point, the Court noted, was that the *Daubert* factors were intended to be applied flexibly. There was no requirement that all four factors be met; rather, the trial judge had discretion to decide which factors were relevant, given the particular case and testimony at hand.

70. *Id.*
71. *Id.* at 158.
72. *Id.* at 147.
73. *Id.* at 148.

With *Kumho Tire*, then, there has been a further expansion of the judge's role in deciding whether to admit expert testimony. As a corollary, there has been a further diminution in the jury's role; yet another area has been shifted from jury to judge decision-making. One of the criticisms that has long been levelled at the jury is that it does not understand technical or scientific evidence. With these three cases, the Supreme Court has limited the expert testimony on scientific, technical, and other specialized knowledge that will reach the jury. For the jury to hear expert testimony on scientific, technical, and other specialized knowledge, the testimony must now meet the threshold requirements identified in *Daubert*, as interpreted by *Joiner*, and as expanded by *Kumho Tire*.

As the judge's role with respect to scientific, technical, and other specialized evidence has expanded, the jury's role has contracted. Under *Frye*, the judge exercised loose control over expert testimony on scientific matters. As long as the experts were well-credentialed and their methods generally accepted, their testimony was admissible, and the jury, as trier of fact, had responsibility for deciding which expert to believe and how much weight to give the testimony. Under the new regime of *Daubert* and its progeny, the judge exercises much greater control than under *Frye*. The effect is that some experts, and even some cases, will no longer make it to the jury, whereas they would have done so under *Frye*. *Daubert* and its progeny not only expand the judge's role, but also limit the jury's role by excluding evidence and even cases that they once would have heard.[74]

74.   Presumably, the jury would have assessed the experts as to their credibility, but not as to the scientific validity of their methods.

CHAPTER 8

JURY DELIBERATIONS

Although the trial judge now has an expanded gatekeeping role when it comes to scientific, technical, and other specialized expert testimony, there is one phase of the trial in which the judge plays a minimal role and the jury assumes the preeminent role and that is during jury deliberations. After both sides have presented their cases and the judge has instructed the jury on the applicable law, the jury retires to the jury room, where it begins its deliberations. Jury deliberations have long been acknowledged to be the province of the jury. Two related features of the deliberations ensure that the jury is autonomous at this stage. The first is that the deliberations are conducted in strict secrecy. The second is that because the deliberations are conducted in secret, the jury is free to structure them however it sees fit, with few guidelines from the court.

Protecting Jury Secrecy

The jury is typically escorted to the jury room by the bailiff. The bailiff informs the jurors that he will be outside the door if they need anything. The jurors are told that if they need to send a note to the judge, they are to do so by having the fore-

147

person hand it to the bailiff. Similarly, if they need
to see an exhibit or ask a question, they are to do so
by having the foreperson make the request to the
judge through the bailiff. The door is closed, and
the jury is shut off from the outside world. The
1957 movie *12 Angry Men*,[1] starring Henry Fonda,
dramatized this moment by having the bailiff lock
the jury room door. This led one juror to remark
somewhat nervously to a fellow juror: "I never
knew they locked the door."[2] The other juror, want-
ing to sound like an experienced juror, responded:
"Sure they lock the door. What'd you think?"[3] But
he was as much taken aback by the procedure as
the first juror. Although the door to most jury
rooms is not actually locked, it is as if it were, given
how isolated the jury becomes during its deliberations.

One reason to have the jury deliberate in secret is
so that jurors feel free to express their views can-
didly with each other. The deliberations are supposed to be a time when jurors, who have sat
through the trial silently and patiently, finally have
the chance to share their reactions. Unless they are
in a courtroom that permits juror questions or
predeliberation discussions,[4] this is their first opportunity to voice their views, misgivings, and confusions. Secrecy during deliberations also means

1. 12 ANGRY MEN (Metro-Goldwyn-Mayer/United Artists
1957).

2. Reginald Rose, Twelve Angry Men 165 (undated unpub-
lished script), *available at* www.scriptshop.com.

3. *Id.*

4. *See supra* Chapter 6.

that jurors can express views that might prove to be unpopular in the larger community. Within the walls of the jury room, however, jurors are free to say what they really think, though their comments should not be so unfiltered that they offend those with whom they are deliberating.

Because jurors' views are not public during deliberations, they also should feel free to change their views. During the deliberations, they are supposed to remain open to each other's arguments and perspectives. Indeed, the judge would have instructed them during the trial to try to keep an open mind; that admonition should guide their deliberations as well. By keeping the jury room door closed and the deliberations secret, it is easier for jurors to change their minds and not feel locked into positions they might have voiced earlier in the deliberations but have since abandoned. They need not worry about how such a shift might appear to others outside the jury room because there are no others, at least at this stage, to learn of it.[5]

Another reason to have the jury deliberate in secret is so that jurors are protected from outside influences. During the deliberations, jurors are physically isolated from all of the other participants in the trial, as well as from the press and the public. What jurors say in the jury room is not supposed to leave the jury room. The idea is that if others knew

5. Juror comments made during deliberations may be revealed in postverdict interviews with the press. For a discussion of the harms and benefits of such interviews, see Nancy S. Marder, *Deliberations and Disclosures: A Study of Post-Verdict Interviews of Jurors*, 82 IOWA L. REV. 465, 489–506 (1997).

what jurors discussed each day, then they might try to influence a juror's views or the direction of the jury's deliberations. Without such knowledge, however, it is more difficult to tamper with the jury and to attempt to influence its deliberations.

As a further precaution in some criminal cases, the court can *sequester* the jury.[6] This means that at the end of each day of deliberation, the jurors will be transported as a group to a hotel, where they will have their meals and spend the night. A marshal is present to limit the jurors' contact with the outside world by screening their telephone calls and the media coverage to which they are exposed. The jurors are not supposed to hear anything about the trial. Again, the goal is to keep the jurors free from outside influence in an effort to ensure that the verdict they reach is one based on the evidence, arguments, and instructions presented at trial and not on the views expressed by friends, family, or legal commentators.

Structuring Jury Deliberations

Other than requiring a foreperson, the court does not usually give the jury any other information as

6. Until recently, for example, all criminal juries in felony cases in New York State courts were sequestered. However, with the jury reforms initiated by Chief Judge Judith Kaye, this practice was eliminated. *See* Somini Sengupta, *New York State Ends the Mandatory Sequestration of Jurors*, N.Y. Times, May 31, 2001, at A20 ("Two years ago, a study by the state court system found that the loosening of the sequestration law [allowing for exceptions in some nonviolent and low-level felonies] resulted in no discernible increase in jury tampering nor in more mistrials. . . . The new law leaves the decision to sequester up to judges at all state trials.").

to how to structure its deliberations. Indeed, the American Judicature Society, an organization that studies the court system and makes recommendations for its improvement, felt the need to fill this gap by creating a pamphlet that, while general in nature, gives jurors a little more information than they currently receive from the court about how to organize their deliberations.[7] For example, the pamphlet offers general advice to the jury on how to begin its deliberations, how to select a foreperson, when to take a vote, how to seek the assistance of the court, and what to do when it has reached an impasse or a verdict.[8]

Selection of a Foreperson

The jury is free to structure its deliberations in any manner it chooses. The only requirement imposed by the court is that one juror serve as foreperson. In some courtrooms, the first juror seated in the jury box is assigned the role of foreperson. In other courtrooms, the judge instructs the jurors to select their own foreperson. According to some studies of mock juries, when the mock jurors select their own foreperson, they usually select someone who is a white, middle-aged man of high status.[9] Often this

7. *See generally* AM. JUDICATURE SOC'Y, BEHIND CLOSED DOORS: A GUIDE FOR JURY DELIBERATIONS (1999).

8. *See id.* at 4–9.

9. *See* REID HASTIE ET AL., INSIDE THE JURY 28 (1983) ("[m]ales, higher classes, and end seating are overrepresented" in the role of foreperson); RITA SIMON, THE JURY AND THE DEFENSE OF INSANITY 114 (1967) (noting that businessmen had a four times better chance of being selected as foreperson than male laborers and that housewives were never selected).

person has chosen to sit at one of the head positions at either end of the rectangular table.[10] One way to increase the chances of being selected as foreperson is to be the juror who asks: "Who wants to be foreperson?" Usually, the other jurors will agree that the person who asks the question should be the foreperson.[11]

At the very least, the foreperson plays an administrative role. The foreperson tallies the votes or writes a note to the judge at the jury's request and hands it to the bailiff when the jury has a question or wants to see an exhibit. The foreperson usually feels some responsibility to move the discussion along and to call for votes at appropriate times. The foreperson can play this role however he or she sees fit, having received scant guidance from the judge as to how it should be fulfilled. As the movie *12 Angry Men* illustrated, the foreperson might simply serve as an administrator. In the movie, the first juror seated in the jury box became the foreperson. The foreperson helped the jury to begin its delibera-

10. *See, e.g.,* KASSIN & WRIGHTSMAN, *supra* note 5 (Ch. 6), at 178 ("Those who sat at the heads of the table were by far the most likely to be chosen...."); LAWRENCE J. SMITH & LORETTA MALANDRO, COURTROOM COMMUNICATION STRATEGIES § 4.47, at 423 (1985) ("Those jurors who sit at the end of the table ... are much more likely to be selected as the foreperson."); Fred Strodtbeck & James Hook, *The Social Dimensions of a Twelve-Man Jury Table,* 24 SOCIOMETRY 397, 400 (1961) (finding that in thirty-two out of sixty-nine experimental jury deliberations, the foreperson was selected from one of the two persons seated at either end of the table).

11. *See* KASSIN & WRIGHTSMAN, *supra* note 5 (Ch. 6), at 178.

tions, suggested taking a vote when the jury appeared stymied in its deliberations, tallied the votes, sent notes to the judge, and tried to quell arguments among the contentious jurors as they arose.

The foreperson in *12 Angry Men*, however, never assumed a position of leadership on the jury, which is a role that a foreperson with high status often plays. In *12 Angry Men*, the leader for the side urging acquittal was an architect, and the leader for the side urging conviction had a seat on the Stock Exchange. In the movie, the foreperson, an assistant high-school football coach, functioned solely in an administrative capacity. In some studies of mock juries, the foreperson participates more than other jurors in the deliberations.[12] He may participate more than other jurors because of his administrative tasks or because he also uses his position to assert his point of view.[13] Other jurors are likely to perceive the foreperson as influential because he participates so actively in the deliberations.[14]

12. *See* SIMON, *supra* note 9, at 114–15 (finding that the mean participation rate of the foreperson was 31.1%, compared to 7.5% for other jurors); Thomas Sannito & Edward Burke Arnolds, *Jury Study Results: The Factors at Work*, 5 TRIAL DIPL. J. 6, 7 (1982) (concluding that from 550 completed juror questionnaires, 79% of jurors described the foreperson as either " 'talkative,' " " 'one of the most talkative,' " or " 'the most talkative' " compared to other jurors).

13. *See* HASTIE ET AL., *supra* note 9, at 145; KASSIN & WRIGHTS-MAN, *supra* note 5 (Ch. 6), at 179.

14. A. Bavelas et al., *Experiments on the Alteration of Group Structure*, 1 J. EXPERIMENTAL SOC. PSYCHOL. 55, 59 (1965) (noting that group members perceived those who spoke the most often as offering the best ideas and guidance).

Styles of Deliberation

Social scientists who have observed mock jury deliberations have identified two styles of deliberation.[15] One style, which they identified as an "evidence-driven deliberation," is when jurors go around the table offering comments about the trial, including the evidence they found the most compelling.[16] At this stage of the deliberations, the jurors try to piece together what happened, with jurors contributing their recollections or interpretations. A public vote is not taken until later in the deliberations.

An actual jury deliberation filmed in state court in Wisconsin serves as an illustration of an evidence-driven deliberation.[17] In that case, Leroy Reed, a man with limited intelligence and a prior felony conviction, was charged with possessing a handgun, in violation of a state law that prohibited convicted felons from possessing firearms. The jury engaged in an evidence-driven deliberation, in which they went around the table so that each juror could give his or her point of view. The jurors did not take a vote until late in the deliberations, after all of the jurors had had a chance to speak and to identify facts and evidence that they thought were important to their assessment of the case. Although some jurors still participated more actively than others, the tone of the deliberations remained civil

15. HASTIE ET AL., *supra* note 9, at 163–65.

16. *Id.*

17. *See Frontline: Inside the Jury Room* transcript (WGBH broadcast), Apr. 8, 1986, at 31–58.

throughout. Toward the end, when one juror, a fireman, was the sole hold-out for conviction, the other jurors remained respectful of his point of view and did not want him to change his vote unless he felt comfortable doing so.

In contrast, another style, which social scientists have identified as a "verdict-driven deliberation," involves a public vote taken almost immediately so that the jurors can see where they stand.[18] As a result of this vote, coalitions form early in the deliberations and jurors align themselves with one coalition or the other. Jurors tend to offer support only for the coalition with which they are aligned. This style of deliberation often leads to participation by a smaller number of jurors than the evidence-driven deliberation, as spokesmen for each position mainly speak. This style of deliberation also can lead to more heated deliberations, as the two sides typically argue in favor of their respective positions.

One reason that jurors choose this style of deliberation is that it appears to them to be efficient. If an initial vote reveals agreement, then the jurors do not have to engage in any further deliberation. If the first vote does not reveal agreement, however, the deliberations that follow can be lengthy and vituperative because the jurors have become wedded to their positions after the initial public vote. Another reason that jurors opt for this style of deliberation is that after sitting through the trial, some jurors have formed a view and they want an

18. *See* HASTIE ET AL., *supra* note 9, at 163–65.

opportunity to announce it. The verdict-driven deliberation, with its call for an initial vote, provides
that opportunity. In addition, an initial vote allows
all jurors to see who must be convinced of what
before there is a verdict. In a sense, it provides
jurors with a snapshot view of how much work is
before them.

The movie *12 Angry Men* serves as an illustration
of a verdict-driven style of deliberation. In the movie, the jurors began their deliberations by taking a
public vote with a show of hands. Coalitions formed
immediately and the tone of the deliberations became hostile, particularly for the lone hold-out,
played by Henry Fonda. However, it takes an un-
usual juror, such as Henry Fonda, to turn the jury
around from an initial vote of eleven to one in
support of conviction to a unanimous vote in support of acquittal. Such a turnaround is rare in real
life. Unless there are several jurors espousing the
same view, the one or two hold-outs usually suc-
cumb to peer pressure.[19]

19. Outcomes like the one in *12 Angry Men*, in which one
juror succeeded in turning around the eleven other jurors, "almost never occur in real life." VALERIE P. HANS & NEIL VIDMAR,
JUDGING THE JURY 110 (1986). Hans and Vidmar note that the
"[p]ressures to conform to the group are strong" and that "[i]t is
only when a minority juror has initial support, in the form of
other jurors with similar views, that the probability that a juror
will sway the majority or hang the jury improves." *Id.; see* KASSIN
& WRIGHTSMAN, *supra* note 5 (Ch. 6), at 182 ("To begin with, the
stor[y] of Henry Fonda ... [is] atypical. The majority almost
always wins."); Rita J. Simon, *Jury Nullification, or Prejudice
and Ignorance in the Marion Barry Trial?*, 20 J. CRIM. JUST. 261,
263 (1992) ("There were no instances [in the data from the
University of Chicago Experimental Jury Project] in which one

Although the evidence-driven style of deliberation is more likely to lead to participation by a greater number of jurors and to a more complete recollection of the facts, courts have resisted telling jurors about these two styles of deliberation, much less recommending one style over the other. The strong view of judges is that jurors should figure this out on their own and opt for the deliberation style that seems right to them. Judges tend to view any greater involvement by the court as an imposition upon the jury's prerogative to structure its deliberations as it sees fit. The American Judicature Society pamphlet makes a move in the right direction when it suggests to jurors that they can "[g]o around the table, one by one, to talk about the case" and "[t]ry to get everyone to talk by saying something like, 'Does anyone else have anything to add?' "[20] Although the pamphlet does not use the labels "evidence-driven" or "verdict-driven," it does suggest to jurors that they follow the evidence-driven style of deliberation by discussing the evidence first before taking a public vote.

There are several advantages to an evidence-driven, rather than a verdict-driven, style of deliberation, which suggest that courts should give some guidance to jurors about deliberation style, whether jurors choose to follow the advice or not. One advantage is that by involving a greater number of jurors in the deliberation, there is a more complete

juror or even two held out against the other ten or eleven and then succeeded in persuading them to adopt their position.").

20. AM. JUDICATURE SOC'Y, *supra* note 7, at 5.

development of the facts and evidence. Some psychologists and social scientists have described the jurors' task as trying to piece together the evidence so that it makes sense, in other words, so that it tells a coherent story.[21] An evidence-driven style of deliberation encourages all of the jurors to participate in this task. If everyone contributes his or her recollections, there will be more information available for group consideration than if just a few jurors dominate the deliberations. Another advantage is that the more cooperative, less hostile, tone also might encourage even shy jurors to participate. As a result, the jury benefits from the recollections, perspectives, and challenges of all twelve jurors (or as close to twelve as possible). The group deliberations, in which jurors can enrich each other's recollections, challenge interpretations, and correct mistaken views, have long been regarded as one of the distinguishing features of a jury trial and one of the advantages of having twelve jurors, rather than a single judge, decide the guilt or innocence of a defendant charged with a serious crime.

Another advantage of an evidence-driven style of deliberation is that it encourages the participation of jurors who would otherwise feel on the margins of the deliberation. The jurors who, because of their race, gender, ethnicity, or even age, worry that their views are not needed or would not be welcome,

21. *See, e.g.,* Nancy Pennington & Reid Hastie, *A Cognitive Theory of Juror Decision Making: The Story Model,* 13 CARDOZO L. REV. 519, 521 (1991) ("[O]ne central claim of the model is that the story the juror constructs determines the juror's decision."); Nancy Pennington & Reid Hastie, *Evidence Evaluation in Complex Decision Making,* 51 PERSONALITY & SOC. PSYCHOL. 242 (1986) (finding that jurors organize trial evidence into a story framework).

might find the evidence-driven style of deliberation more conducive to their participation. For example, studies of the deliberations of mock juries and small groups indicate that men's participation rate in such settings is proportionately greater than that of women.[22] Although women's roles in society have undergone much change since a number of these studies were conducted, the patterns of participation based on gender have not changed significantly.[23] Thus, a style of deliberation, such as the evidence-driven style, which is more inclusive, could encourage greater participation from jurors, and in particular from women, who might be more restrained in voicing their views.

Race is another basis on which jurors might feel more or less likely to participate in the deliberations. As the filmed jury deliberation in the Wisconsin state court revealed, the sole African-American man on that jury felt on the periphery of the deliberations and expressed and demonstrated that view to his fellow jurors. He told the other jurors that he would accede to whatever view the majority took[24] and then he literally left the table where the

22. *See* Nancy S. Marder, Note, *Gender Dynamics and Jury Deliberations*, 96 YALE L.J. 593, 595–97 (1987).

23. *See, e.g.*, Priscilla M. Elsass & Laura M. Graves, *Demographic Diversity in Decision-Making Groups: The Experiences of Women and People of Color*, 22 ACAD. MGMT. REV. 946, 947 (1997) ("In diverse groups interactions between members may reflect existing norms, creating barriers to the full participation of women and people of color.").

24. *See Frontline: Inside the Jury Room* transcript, *supra* note 17, at 16 ("Like I said, I feel I'm on shaky ground here, and

jurors were seated and walked to another part of the jury room where he remained for much of the deliberations. Even though the Wisconsin jury engaged in an evidence-driven style of deliberation, it was not enough to persuade this juror to participate fully in the deliberations. Although an evidence-driven style of deliberation might not, in the end, persuade all jurors to participate, it is at least a starting-point. A diverse jury is key to both a wide range of perspectives being made available to the jury and to the larger community's acceptance of the jury verdict. If jurors do not feel comfortable expressing their views, then the diversity of the jury will be in name only.

Contributing Different Perspectives

Whether jurors choose a verdict-driven or evidence-driven style of deliberation, it is important that all of the jurors feel comfortable contributing their views so that the jury benefits from as many different perspectives as possible. The U.S. Supreme Court justices have expressed differing views on the importance of having a range of perspectives available to the jury. This discussion has usually been framed in terms of the venire and why it is important that the venire be drawn from a fair cross-section of the community.

According to some justices, such as Chief Justice Rehnquist and Justice Scalia, as long as the jurors selected from the venire are impartial, that is all

I'm willing to go with the majority because I'm not—I'm not strong on my stance so I—this is one time I need help.'') (quoting juror Henry Arvin).

the U.S. Constitution requires. These justices are not concerned with whether there is an array of perspectives available to the jury during its deliberations. Rather, they are concerned only with whether twelve, impartial jurors have been drawn from the venire and seated on the petit jury. For this reason, then Justice Rehnquist, writing in dissent in *Taylor v. Louisiana*,[25] thought that there was no constitutional violation if women were systematically excluded from the venire. He explained that the systematic exclusion of women from the venire was no more a constitutional violation than the systematic exclusion of doctors or lawyers, who were exempted from jury service in a number of states.[26] In his view, the Sixth Amendment required only that defendant Taylor be tried by an impartial and unbiased jury.

Other justices, such as Justices Marshall, White, and Douglas, explained that a venire should be drawn from a fair cross-section of the community so that a range of perspectives is available to the jury during its deliberations. They did not mean that people of a particular race or gender would hold a particular view or vote in a particular way. Rather, they meant that people of different races, genders, or other background characteristics might have had different experiences that would shape the way that they saw the facts or evidence of the case. Each of these justices explained in his own way that the connection between one's race or gender could not

25.   419 U.S. 522 (1975).

26.   *See id.* at 542 (Rehnquist, J., dissenting).

be used to predict one's views, but rather, the connection was more subtle and complex. In *Ballard v. United States*,[27] Justice Douglas surmised that the systematic exclusion of women from the venire, like the exclusion of men, would lead to a paucity of views for the jury to consider during its deliberations:

> [I]f the shoe were on the other foot, who would claim that a jury was truly representative of the community if all men were intentionally and systematically excluded from the panel? The truth is that the two sexes are not fungible; a community made up exclusively of one is different from a community composed of both; the subtle interplay of influence one on the other is among the imponderables. To insulate the courtroom from either may not in a given case make an iota of difference. Yet a flavor, a distinct quality is lost if either sex is excluded.[28]

In *Peters v. Kiff*,[29] Justice Marshall described the loss that would ensue if African-American jurors were systematically excluded from the venire, even in a case in which the defendant was a white man: "When any large and identifiable segment of the community is excluded from jury service, the effect is to remove from the jury room qualities of human nature and varieties of human experience, the

27.   329 U.S. 187 (1946) (relying on the supervisory powers of the federal courts, the Court held that the exclusion of women from the venire was impermissible).

28.   *Id.* at 193–94 (footnote omitted).

29.   407 U.S. 493 (1972).

range of which is unknown and perhaps unknowable."[30] In his view, people of different backgrounds contribute different perspectives in ways that are unknowable but nevertheless significant. If, for example, the venire excludes African-American men or all women, their experiences and perspectives will be lost to the petit jury.

In *Taylor v. Louisiana*,[31] Justice White built upon the language and insights in both *Ballard* and *Peters* to conclude that the systematic exclusion of women from the venire violated a defendant's Sixth Amendment right to a jury drawn from a fair cross-section of the community. Writing in 1975, he noted that women "are sufficiently numerous and distinct from men" that their exclusion from the venire violates the fair cross-section requirement.[32] In *Taylor*, Justice White echoed the view voiced by Justice Douglas in *Ballard* that men and women might have different perspectives and make different contributions in the jury room so that the systematic exclusion of women from the venire could result in the loss of valuable perspectives during deliberations.[33]

The Court was circumspect, particularly in *Peters* and *Taylor*, about how far its view extended. While the venire must be broadly drawn from the community so that different views will be available to the jury during its deliberations, the Court did not

30. *Id.* at 503.

31. 419 U.S. 522 (1975).

32. *Id.* at 531.

33. *Id.* at 531–33.

mandate that the petit jury actually consist of jurors with a wide range of perspectives. In addition, although the Court held in *Peters v. Kiff*[34] that African-American men could not be systematically excluded from the venire and in *Taylor v. Louisiana*[35] that women could not be similarly excluded, the Court did not go so far as to conclude that the petit jury had to mirror the community; in fact, it believed that such a position would be untenable.[36]

Requiring Unanimity

When jurors do speak during deliberations, their fellow jurors need to listen. One way to ensure that all of the different perspectives on the jury are heard is to require a unanimous verdict. Anything less than unanimity means that the juror who voices a dissenting view does not have to be taken seriously, and can even be ignored by his fellow jurors. In contrast, a unanimity requirement fosters deliberations, particularly if there is at least one dissenting juror. The other jurors need to win over the juror or jurors taking a minority view, and, in doing so, the jury is likely to engage in a thorough discussion of the facts and evidence. In other words, the unanimity requirement is one way to foster group deliberations, and a group deliberation is one

34. 407 U.S. at 505.

35. 419 U.S. at 537.

36. *See id.* at 538 ("It should also be emphasized that in holding that petit juries must be drawn from a source fairly representative of the community we impose no requirement that petit juries actually chosen must mirror the community....").

of the key features that distinguishes the jury from other decision-makers.

To return to the example of the movie *12 Angry Men*, if there had not been a unanimity requirement, the jurors could have entered the jury room, taken a vote, seen that it was eleven to one in favor of conviction, and immediately returned a guilty verdict without ever having deliberated. The conviction would have resulted in the death of the defendant because the death penalty was mandatory in that state. However, because the jury had to reach a unanimous verdict, the jurors had to engage in further deliberations. Henry Fonda, with his lone vote for acquittal, had managed to slow down the deliberative process. In doing so, Fonda had the opportunity to explain what troubled him about the prosecutor's evidence. Admittedly, it is rare in life, though not in the movies, for a single juror to convince the remaining eleven to take his position.[37] Usually a juror needs the support of at least two or three others to accomplish such a turnaround,[38] but "it's possible,"[39] as Henry Fonda was fond of saying whenever he suggested a new interpretation of the evidence.

37. Outcomes like the one in *12 Angry Men* "almost never occur in real life." HANS & VIDMAR, *supra* note 19, at 110.

38. Research has shown that the "[p]ressures to conform to the group are strong" and "[i]t is only when a minority juror has initial support, in the form of other jurors with similar views, that the probability that a juror will sway the majority or hang the jury improves." *Id.*

39. Rose, *supra* note 2, at 203.

Whether a unanimous verdict is required varies from federal to state courts and from criminal to civil cases. In federal court, in both civil and criminal cases, the verdict must be unanimous.[40] However, a criminal case in federal court requires a unanimous verdict by a jury consisting of twelve jurors,[41] whereas a civil case in federal court requires a unanimous verdict by a jury consisting of six to twelve jurors.[42] Clearly, it is more difficult to obtain unanimity among twelve jurors than it is among six. Yet, many federal court judges have become comfortable with civil juries typically consisting of six to eight jurors.[43] This practice has become commonplace because of its perceived efficiency.

Although practices in state courts vary, in many state courts, just as in federal court, a criminal jury typically consists of twelve jurors and the jury must reach a unanimous verdict.[44] There are several policy reasons to require a unanimous verdict by a criminal jury, though not all states have this requirement. One reason is to make it difficult to achieve a conviction because so much is at stake, namely, the liberty or life of the defendant. The reasonable doubts of just one juror are enough to lead to a hung jury under a unanimity requirement.

40. *See* FED. R. CIV. P. 48; FED. R. CRIM. P. 31.

41. *See* FED. R. CRIM. P. 23(b).

42. *See* FED. R. CIV. P. 48.

43. *See* Improving Jury Selection and Juror Comprehension, *supra* note 36 (Ch. 3).

44. *See* Marder, *supra* note 15 (Ch. 3), at 945 n.308 (listing states that require a unanimous verdict in criminal jury trials).

A second reason is because the criminal jury speaks for the community-at-large; thus, even when the verdict is one with which the larger community disagrees, it is more likely to accept the verdict if it was reached by all twelve jurors rather than by just a majority. A third reason is to ensure that all of the jurors, no matter how diverse their backgrounds, have come to agreement in the case of the defendant. A unanimous verdict ensures that all jurors are listened to during the deliberations and that no juror's views or vote are ignored. Furthermore, if a jury drawn from a broad swath of the community can agree unanimously that the defendant is guilty, that should reassure the defendant and the community that the verdict has been carefully considered by those who might view the case from very different vantage points.

In many state courts, civil juries are typically smaller than criminal juries (six to eight jurors rather than twelve) and do not require a unanimous verdict.[45] The greater protections afforded to a criminal defendant make sense in light of what is at stake for him. Although a civil verdict can have serious consequences for a party, such as social stigma or the loss of money, the repercussions are not as serious as those faced by the criminal defendant who could suffer loss of liberty or life. Thus, the balance has been struck slightly differently for civil juries than for criminal juries. The number of jurors required on a civil jury is not always as high

45. *See* Improving Jury Selection and Juror Comprehension, *supra* note 36 (Ch. 3).

and the level of agreement the jurors must reach is not always as great because these requirements impose costs. Additional jurors will add to the cost of the trial and the larger jury could lead to lengthier deliberations. However, in spite of the cost-saving of smaller juries, the Supreme Court held in *Ballew v. Georgia*[46] that a criminal jury cannot consist of fewer than six jurors, and the reasoning the Court relied on in *Ballew* is equally applicable to a civil jury. The *Ballew* Court, relying on numerous empirical studies by academics,[47] concluded that a jury consisting of fewer than six persons might impair jury fact-finding, be more susceptible to individual biases and group errors, produce more inconsistent and unreliable verdicts, make hung juries less likely to occur, and lead to less minority representation on juries; in contrast, the administrative savings (court time and money) are likely to be de minimis.[48]

Between *Williams v. Florida*,[49] decided in 1970, and *Ballew*, decided in 1978,[50] a number of academics had entered the debate[51] and highlighted two trends that seemed to be in conflict with each other. At a time when jury service was being extended to more of the population than ever before,

46. 435 U.S. 223 (1978).

47. *See id.* at 232 n.10.

48. *See id.* at 232–44.

49. 399 U.S. 78 (1970).

50. 435 U.S. 223 (1978).

51. *See, e.g., Ballew*, 435 U.S. at 232 n.10 (listing some of the empirical studies on which the Court relied).

thus creating the potential for truly diverse juries, courts were reducing jury size and replacing unanimity decision rules with majority decision rules, thus potentially disenfranchising the very jurors whose participation had only recently been sought.

One effect of reduced jury size would be to limit jury diversity. If only six jurors rather than twelve were required, for example, it was more likely that the six would be a less diverse mix than the twelve. Similarly, if the six were less representative of the larger population than twelve, there was a greater chance that they would return a verdict that did not accord with the larger community's views. At the same time, if the smaller juries could ignore some of their members' views because they were not required for a majority decision, then there was even less of a check on the jury and a greater chance that the jury verdict would not reflect the views of the larger community.

Much of the debate that took place in the 1970s on these two related questions of decision rule and jury size has subsided. In part, this may be because the Supreme Court has set a floor below which the number of jurors on a criminal jury cannot fall— six-person juries in criminal cases whether in federal or state court—and gave reasons for its decision that apply equally to civil juries. In part, this may be because much of the experimentation with smaller jury size and relaxed decision rules has taken place in civil rather than criminal cases. When trade-offs have been made in the name of greater efficiency, they have mainly affected civil juries. In addition, judges have now had experience in working with the smaller juries and have not noticed deleterious effects. Although my own view, and that of several other commentators,[52] is that the larger, twelve-person juries are preferable to the smaller juries and that a unanimity requirement is preferable to a majority rule, the need for greater efficiency has meant that the twelve-person jury and unanimity requirement have not always prevailed.

From time to time, however, particularly after a high-profile criminal trial in which the defendant was not convicted,[53] there has been a renewed call to abandon the unanimity requirement and to replace it with an 11–1 or 10–2 decision rule in criminal cases. This occurred in California, for example, after O.J. Simpson was acquitted of state criminal charges.[54] Yet, ironically, the legislation

52. *See, e.g., Ballew*, 435 U.S. at 232 n.10 (listing many academics whose empirical work supported the continuation of twelve-person juries); Diamond, *supra* note 37 (Ch. 3), at 317 (recommending a return to twelve-person juries in civil jury trials).

53. One jury scholar, Professor Valerie Hans, has noted that public dissatisfaction with juries may stem from a "very strong" belief that "courts are not doing enough to punish wrongdoers." Laura Mansnerus, *Under Fire, Jury System Faces Overhaul*, N.Y. TIMES, Nov. 4, 1995, at A9 (quoting Prof. Hans). Recent cases that incensed the public, such as "Rodney King, Bobbitt, Menendez, [and] Simpson" were all "prodefendant decision[s]," and in Professor Hans' view, would not have been as controversial "if these juries were convicting." *Id.*

54. *See, e.g., California Blue Ribbon Panel Urges Wide Range of Jury Reforms*, WEST'S LEGAL NEWS, May 3, 1996, *available in* 1996 WL 260677 (announcing the Judicial Council's Blue Ribbon Commission proposals for jury reform, which included a recom-

that was proposed,[55] though not passed, in response to the Simpson acquittal would not have affected the very jury that had inspired it because the Simpson criminal jury reached a unanimous verdict.

Responding to Hung Juries

The O.J. Simpson acquittal also sparked a debate about hung juries and whether they have increased in number, even though the Simpson jury was not a hung jury. There was a growing public sentiment, perhaps stemming from the growing diversity of juries and the writings of some academics[56] or the lobbying of some prosecutors, that more juries were failing to reach a verdict than in the past. There was also a sense that it was minority jurors who

mendation for nonanimous verdicts); Greg Krikorian, *Committee Hearing a Trial by Fire for the Jury System*, L.A. TIMES, July 28, 1995, at 3 (describing a proposal by State Senator Charles Calderon, Chair of the Senate Judiciary Committee, which "would allow 11–1 verdicts in all but capital cases"); *Wilson Touts Jury Reform, Cites Simpson Trial*, L.A. DAILY NEWS, July 18, 1995, at N4, *available in* 1995 WL 5411715 ("[Former Governor Pete] Wilson told a group of prosecuting attorneys . . . that he supports a bill . . . that would allow criminal convictions on a 10–2 vote of jurors in all but death penalty cases.").

55. *See, e.g.,* Assembly Const. Amend. 18, 1995 Cal. Sess.; Senate Const. Amend. 24, 1995 Cal. Sess.

56. *See, e.g.,* Paul Butler, *Racially Based Jury Nullification: Black Power in the Criminal Justice System*, 105 YALE L.J. 677 (1995) (urging African-American jurors to nullify when African-American defendants were charged with nonviolent, victimless crimes, so that there would be more hung juries and perhaps fewer African-American men being sent to jail); Jeffrey Rosen, *One Angry Woman*, NEW YORKER, Feb. 24 & Mar. 3, 1997, at 54 (criticizing hung juries and suggesting that African-American women were refusing to deliberate in order to create more hung juries so that fewer African-American men would be sent to jail).

were using the jury box to cast a lone vote for acquittal, thus registering their disapproval with the criminal justice system and creating hung juries that could ultimately result in the defendant going free.

What Is a Hung Jury?

A hung jury is one in which the jury does not reach the level of agreement needed to satisfy whichever decision rule is in place. A hung jury can result in either a civil or criminal case in either state court or federal court. For example, if a criminal jury needs to reach a unanimous verdict, and eleven jurors vote to convict and one juror votes to acquit, and the dissenting juror is unwilling to change his or her vote even after further deliberation by the jury and instruction from the judge, then that jury is likely to be declared a hung jury. It remains for the judge to decide whether the jury has deliberated for a sufficient amount of time. If the judge concludes that the jury has, and if the jury continues to report to the judge that no further progress is possible, then the judge will declare a hung jury. Once the judge declares a hung jury, it remains for the prosecution to decide whether to retry the case before a new jury.

Ways of Responding to a Jury That Has Reached Impasse

The jury is able to decide in the first instance if it has reached an impasse. The judge never informs the jury beforehand that this is a possibility. Typically, however, when a jury is heading toward an impasse, the jurors realize at some point in their deliberations that they have become entrenched in their positions and that they are not making any progress toward achieving the vote they need for a verdict. When they have reached this point, one of the jurors usually suggests that the foreperson send a note to the judge informing the judge that the jury has reached an impasse.

The traditional response of the judge to a jury that has reported that it has reached an impasse is to deliver what is known as an "*Allen* charge."[57] In this charge, the judge instructs the jury to go back to the jury room, to engage in further deliberations, and to try to reach a verdict. Although the judge does not tell the jurors to compromise on their vote, jurors often arrive at a compromise, and ultimately, return a verdict. Defense attorneys worry that the *Allen* charge puts pressure on a jury to return a verdict when it otherwise would have been declared a hung jury. For the defendant, the difference between a verdict and a hung jury can be the difference between conviction and freedom (assuming the prosecutor decides not to retry the case).

Some state court judges have experimented with another response to a jury that has reached an impasse: the judge meets with the jury, discusses the problem, and decides whether additional argu-

57. In such a charge, approved in *Allen v. United States*, 164 U.S. 492 (1896), the judge usually "remind[s the jurors] of the nature of their duty and the time and expense of a trial, and urg[es] them to try again to reach a verdict." United States v. Anderton, 679 F.2d 1199, 1203 (5th Cir. 1982) (citations omitted).

ment by the attorneys would help the jury to overcome its impasse.[58] If the jury is able to identify the
point that has led to the standstill, and the attorneys are able to address this point, the theory is
that the jury will be able to reach a verdict. This
judge-jury "dialogue" to try to figure out if the
judge or attorneys can help the jury in some way
has been implemented in Arizona state courts.[59]
One question this dialogue raises is whether the
judge should play this more intrusive role in the
deliberations because the deliberations are the ex-
clusive province of the jury. One answer, though, is
that the judge has been invited to intrude by the
jury. Another answer is that the judge already plays
an intrusive role by delivering an *Allen* charge, and
that the judge-jury dialogue is more narrowly tailored to address the particular sticking point for the
jury than the blunt, boilerplate instruction provided
by the *Allen* charge.

The judge-jury dialogue, as well as other jury
reforms implemented in Arizona state courts, has
served as a catalyst for several academic studies on
hung juries. One study, which used data from Ari-

58. Judges in Arizona are now experimenting with an alternative to the *Allen* charge; they are speaking to juries that have
reached an impasse and trying to see how they can help. *See* THE
POWER OF 12, *supra* note 39 (Ch. 3), at 120–22; Dann & Logan,
supra note 19 (Ch. 7), at 283 (describing some of Arizona's more
controversial jury reforms, including having the judge and jury
engage in a dialogue if the jury has reached an impasse to see if
the judge or attorneys can provide the jury with additional
information).

59. *See, e.g.*, Margaret A. Jacobs, *Arizona Supreme Court
Approves Major Changes in Jury Practices*, WALL ST. J., Nov. 2,
1995, at B12.

zona and three other jurisdictions, examined jurors' views about legal fairness in an effort to understand when jurors who served on hung juries might have engaged in nullification.[60] Another study focused on hung jury rates at these same locations, including Arizona.[61] This study reported that the hung-jury rate had not increased significantly since Professor Harry Kalven and Professor Hans Zeisel's 1966 landmark study, *The American Jury*.[62] In that early empirical work, Kalven and Zeisel found that only about five percent of the jury trials in their study produced hung juries.[63] Although the recent study on hung juries assuaged fears about a rise in today's hung-jury rates, the more difficult, and still unanswered, question is: What is the "right" number of hung juries?

The Value of Hung Juries

Hung juries play an essential, albeit unappreciated, role in our jury system. They show respect for the individual juror and his or her views. Although judges instruct jurors to keep an open mind and to listen to the views of their fellow jurors, in the end, jurors must vote consistent with their own best judgment. No juror should be coerced or pressured

60. *See* Paula L. Hannaford-Agor & Valerie P. Hans, *Nullification at Work? A Glimpse From the National Center for State Courts Study of Hung Juries*, 78 CHI.-KENT L. REV. 1249 (2003).

61. *See* Paula L. Hannaford-Agor et al., *Are Hung Juries a Problem?*, *available at* http://www.ncsconline.org (posted on Sept. 30, 2002).

62. HARRY KALVEN, JR. & HANS ZEISEL, THE AMERICAN JURY (1966).

63. *Id.* at 56 (finding that in a sample of 3576 criminal trials in 1955–56 and 1958, 5.5% resulted in hung juries).

into changing his or her vote. In fact, it is far easier to go along with the other jurors than it is to be a hold-out and to know that one's vote is standing in the way of a verdict that eleven other jurors believe is correct. Yet, it is the responsibility of the individual juror to vote consistent with his or her conscience. Although the jury deliberations do not make it easy for the hold-out to withstand group pressure, should the hold-out do so, the result will be a hung jury. Although prosecutors may look upon that result as a failure of the system, academics and judges have long regarded it as one of the system's strengths. Almost thirty-five years ago, Professor Zeisel described the hung jury as a "treasured, paradoxical phenomenon."[64] He explained that the hung jury is "treasured because it represents the legal system's respect for the minority viewpoint that is held strongly enough to thwart the will of the majority" and it is paradoxical because the hung jury can only be tolerated in "moderation"—"too many hung juries would impede the effective functioning of the courts."[65]

Of course, if too many cases result in hung juries, the system would break down. As long as the hung jury is reserved for those cases in which one or more jurors truly believe that to vote otherwise would be inconsistent with their responsibilities as jurors, then the hung jury plays a critical role in allowing jurors to express their strongly held judg-

64. Hans Zeisel, ... *And Then There Were None: The Diminution of the Federal Jury*, 38 U. Chi. L. Rev. 710, 719 (1971).

65. *Id.* at 719 n.42.

ment about a case. Were it otherwise, jurors would feel that they are being asked to vote against their own best judgment. As one juror noted, citizens do not fulfil their responsibilities as jurors if they vote in a mechanical, computer-like way.[66] According to this juror, citizens serve as jurors in order to do justice;[67] if they do anything less, they could simply be replaced by computers.

Jurors need to be able to live with their votes after their jury service has ended. In one jury trial in Arizona in which the deliberations were filmed and aired on national television, one juror who ended up creating a hung jury explained that he was voting in the only way he could because he had to be able to live with his vote for the rest of his life.[68] Although the possibility of a hung jury allows jurors to live with themselves afterward, a hung jury does not mean that the hold-out juror's vote determines the defendant's fate. In the case of the Arizona jury, for example, the defendant was re-tried before a new jury, which quickly convicted

66. *See Frontline: Inside the Jury Room* transcript, *supra* note 17, at 11 ("I am not a computer, and I will not accept everything that[] I'm told for—just because I am told that—that it is true. I can't do that as a thinking, breathing, human being.") (quoting Juror Lester Sauvage).

67. *Id.* at 15 ("I'm trying to decide in my own mind—has justice been done here?") (quoting Juror Lester Sauvage).

68. *CBS Reports: Enter the Jury Room* transcript (CBS broadcast), Apr. 16, 1997, at 49 ("I was not going to do something that was against my beliefs and conscience and logic that would make me regret what I had done for the rest of my life.") (quoting juror identified as Joe).

him.[69]

In spite of the noble purpose behind the hung jury, there is a thin line between the hung juror who votes his or her conscience and the obstreperous juror who closes his or her mind to reasonable persuasion. Because jury deliberations are conducted in secret, as discussed earlier,[70] it is often difficult for those outside the jury room to know whether the hung jury was the result of the noble juror voting his or her conscience or the recalcitrant juror refusing to deliberate. In light of such difficulties, prosecutors, the press, and the public tend to see the hung jury in a negative light. They focus on the resources required to bring the trial in the first place, and the added resources that must be expended should the prosecutor decide to retry the case. This issue has been in the limelight in a recent spate of high-profile cases, such as the trial of Frank Quattrone, a banker at Credit Suisse First Boston, whose first trial for obstruction of justice ended in a hung jury.[71]

Interpreting Nullification

The hung jury, though open to differences in interpretation and to disagreements about how many hung juries are too many for the system to bear, is less controversial than the nullifying jury. One way to view the nullifying jury is as an exten-

69. *See id.* at 57.

70. *See supra* text accompanying notes 1–6.

71. *See* Andrew Ross Sorkin, *Evidence Barred in Banker Retrial; E-Mails Suggest that Credit Suisse Kept Quattrone in the Dark*, INTERNAT'L HERALD TRIB., Apr. 13, 2003, at 13.

sion of the hung jury and the respect accorded to the individual juror to vote consistent with his or her conscience. Although this is the view I take, it remains a minority view. The traditional view is that there is a sharp demarcation between a nullifying jury, which has decided not to follow the law, and a hung jury, which is adhering to the law but simply cannot reach agreement. According to the traditional view, there is a divide between the hung jury (law-abiding) and the nullifying jury (law-defying) which should not be crossed. Instead, I see a continuum in which both hung juries and nullifying juries have engaged in considered deliberations (law-regarding) and serve a critical function as safety valves in the legal system.

What Is Jury Nullification?

Jury nullification is when the jury chooses not to follow the law as it has been explained by the judge to the jury. Nullification can be distinguished from mistake, which is when the jury fails to follow the law because it has simply misunderstood it. With nullification, the jury has knowingly chosen not to follow the law for any of several reasons.

Juries can engage in nullification because they are usually asked to return a general verdict ("guilty" or "not guilty" in criminal cases; "liable" or "not liable" in civil cases), making it difficult for those outside the jury room to know the basis for the jury's decision. Theoretically, a jury can nullify in a civil or a criminal case, but in a civil case, the judge can limit the jury's opportunity by requiring the jury to reach its verdict through a series of questions (special verdict or interrogatories),[72] rather than a general verdict alone, or the judge can override the general verdict (judgment as a matter of law) if the judge believes it is not supported by the evidence.[73] In a criminal case, a jury can nullify when returning a conviction or an acquittal, but if the jury chooses the former, the judge can override (judgment of acquittal)[74] it, though as a matter of practice, judges are hesitant to do so. However, when a jury nullifies and acquits, the verdict stands and is not appealable. This is because the Double Jeopardy Clause of the Fifth Amendment to the U.S. Constitution[75] precludes retrial by the same sovereign once the defendant has been acquitted.

There are basically three instances in which a jury nullifies. One is when a jury disagrees with the law. In such a case, the jury understands that the law was passed by the legislature and is supposed to be applied, but the jury disagrees with the law and expresses its disagreement by failing to apply the law to the case before it. This type of nullification was common during Prohibition, when many juries refused to apply the law that banned the sale of

72. *See* FED. R. CIV. P. 49 (Special Verdicts and Interrogatories).

73. *See* FED. R. CIV. P. 50 (Judgment as a Matter of Law in Jury Trials).

74. *See* FED. R. CRIM. P. 29 (Motion for Judgment of Acquittal).

75. The Fifth Amendment provides in relevant part: "[N]or shall any person be subject for the same offence to be twice put in jeopardy of life or limb." U.S. CONST. amend. V.

alcohol.[76] Eventually, after much public disagreement and many jury acquittals, the law was repealed.[77] Thus, one purpose served by this type of nullification is that if enough juries register their disagreement with a law, they signal to the other branches of government the need to take action. Although juries do not change the law, they can indicate to the legislature that the law needs to be changed. Or they can indicate to the executive branch (the prosecutor) the need to enforce the law in a different way. Of course, juries may nullify because they disagree with a law, but a majority of the citizenry might still favor the law. For example, a jury may believe that abortion is wrong and refuse to apply the ban that limits how close abortion protestors can stand to an abortion clinic even though Congress has passed a statute, the Freedom of Access to Clinic Entrances Act (FACE),[78] which prohibits abortion protestors from preventing access to abortion clinics and which has the support of a majority of voters in the country.

A second instance in which a jury nullifies is when it does not think the law should be applied to the particular defendant. With this type of nullification, the jury agrees with the law, thinks it is a good law, but does not think the law should be applied to the defendant in the case before it. The

76. *See* Alan Scheflin & Jon Van Dyke, *Jury Nullification: The Contours of a Controversy*, 43 LAW & CONTEMP. PROBS., Autumn 1980, at 51, 71.

77. *See* U.S. CONST. amend. XXI, § 1 (repealing the Eighteenth Amendment).

78. *See* 18 U.S.C.A. § 248 (West Supp. 1998).

jury in *Inside the Jury Room* nullified for this reason.[79] This jury agreed with the Wisconsin law that convicted felons should not be allowed to possess firearms, but it did not think that the law should be applied to Leroy Reed, a man of limited intelligence and good intentions, who had purchased a gun in order to complete a mail-order course to become a detective. When Leroy Reed was questioned by the sheriff about why he was standing on the courthouse steps, he explained that he was looking for clients; he even volunteered to go home and bring his gun to the sheriff, which he eventually did. The jury in Reed's case nullified because it believed that the law was not meant to include defendants such as Reed, and that the jury's job was to do justice, not just to apply the statute mechanically.[80]

Of course, juries also can nullify and acquit defendants for far more ignominious reasons, such as racial prejudice. For example, all-white juries in the South refused to apply the criminal laws to whites charged with serious crimes against African Americans; instead, they nullified and the white defendants went free.[81]

A third instance in which a jury nullifies is to send a message about a social problem that extends

79. *See Frontline: Inside the Jury Room* transcript, *supra* note 17, at 22 ("What we're saying is this trial shouldn't even have been brought....") (quoting Juror Karl Buetow); *id.* ("I think that's the consensus around the room.") (quoting Foreperson James Pepper).

80. *Id.* at 11 (quoting Juror Lester Sauvage).

81. *See* Marder, *supra* note 15 (Ch. 3), at 888–90.

beyond the particular case before it. For example, a jury might use nullification to express its disagreement with the criminal justice system in general or with the criminal justice system's treatment of African Americans in particular. Nullification is less effective as a means of indicating general dissatisfaction with a larger societal problem, especially one outside the courtroom, because the message is often difficult to discern and the societal problem is often difficult to correct, especially through the court system. The higher-than-average acquittal rates in criminal cases, especially in drug cases, in certain cities, such as the Bronx, New York and Washington, D.C., might be examples of this type of nullification.[82] However, the higher-than-average acquittal rates in these areas also may be the result of juries consisting largely of African Americans who have a greater distrust of police and who are more willing to question the reliability of their testimony than white jurors.[83] Thus, the acquittals in these cities could be the result of reasonable doubt rather than nullification.

Why Nullification Raises Concerns

One reason that nullification raises concerns among judges, prosecutors, legislators, and the public is that it is an example of citizens, who in their official capacity as jurors, have disregarded the law.

82. *See id.* at 899–901.

83. *See* Roger Parloff, *Race and Juries: If It Ain't Broke,* A.B.A.J., June 1997, at 5, 6 (suggesting that Bronx juries are not acquitting at unusually high rates, but are merely at the high end of the norm).

The legal system is based upon adherence to the rule of law, and jurors who nullify appear to ignore this central tenet. This not only threatens the legal system, but also encroaches upon the roles performed by the other branches of government.

Judges who write about jury nullification often describe it as leading to "anarchy and chaos."[84] Jurors, like judges and prosecutors, have taken an oath to uphold the law; when jurors nullify, they ostensibly are failing to abide by their oath. If decision-makers, such as juries and judges, fail to follow the law, and instead, apply it in an arbitrary manner, then parties, and the public-at-large, will lose faith in the system. Judges often regard jury nullification as the first step down the slippery slope that will lead to the undoing of the legal system.

Judges also regard jury nullification with unease because they see it as an instance of the jury overstepping its proper role. The traditional view is that the judge's role is to instruct the jurors on the relevant law. According to this view, the jurors' role is to apply the law, as the judge gives it to them, to the facts as the jury finds them. When a jury nullifies, it is doing something more than just finding the facts and applying the law. While judges view jury nullification as an encroachment upon the judicial function, legislators view it as a usurpation

---

84. *See, e.g.,* United States v. Dougherty, 473 F.2d 1113, 1133 (D.C. Cir. 1972) ("This so-called right of jury nullification is put forward in the name of liberty and democracy, but its explicit avowal risks the ultimate logic of anarchy....").

of the legislative function. The legislature's job is to enact statutes. The legislature is considered the appropriate body to perform this task because it represents the views of a majority of the electorate. When a jury nullifies, it does not change the law; only the legislature can do that. But a jury that nullifies fails to follow the law that the legislature intended to be applied across-the-board. If a statute does not do what it was intended to do, then it is the legislature's job to amend or repeal it; it is not the job of a small group of unelected jurors to try to correct what they perceive as a problem with the legislation.

The executive branch, as represented by the prosecutor, has the task of enforcing the law; jury nullification runs counter to the prosecutor's mission as well. During voir dire, the prosecutor is likely to ask prospective jurors whether they can follow the law, and they are likely to say that they can. Before serving on the petit jury, jurors also would have taken an oath in which they swore to follow the law. Prosecutors try to gain commitments from jurors that they will follow the law. Once they have gained these commitments, they expect them to be followed; nullification appears to be a disavowal of these commitments. Once the prosecutor has decided to bring a case, and has presented evidence establishing a defendant's guilt beyond a reasonable doubt, the prosecutor expects a conviction. Anything less than this appears to fly in the face of the law, and that is exactly what nullification appears to do from the prosecutor's perspective.

Members of the public, who believe the law represents their views and was enacted on their behalf, wonder how a small group of twelve people can fail to apply the law that was passed in the name of the larger community by a legislative body that is far more representative than an individual jury. The portrayal of the nullifying jury in the popular press is of a jury that has flouted the law. After the acquittal of O.J. Simpson of state criminal charges, the press not only speculated that the jury had engaged in nullification, even though jurors claimed in postverdict interviews that they had had reasonable doubt, but also used the term as a way of disparaging the verdict reached by a jury consisting largely of African Americans.[85]

The Benefits of Nullification

Although the popular image of nullification is of a jury gone awry, this portrayal fails to capture the positive roles that jury nullification plays in the legal system. Nullification provides several benefits: it allows one branch of government to give feedback to the other branches; it allows jurors to render a verdict consistent with their sense of justice; and it offers a broader conception of the role of the jury that is closer to the role juries actually play than that provided by the traditional view.

85. *See* Nancy S. Marder, *The Interplay of Race and False Claims of Jury Nullification*, 32 U. MICH. J.L. REFORM 285 (1999).

Nullification as Feedback. Juries, along with judges, constitute the judiciary, one of the three branches of government. Jury nullification is a way in which juries can signal to the other two branches of government the need for a change in the law. The change can either be in the law itself, which would require legislative action, or in the way the law is being enforced, which would require executive action. Although the jury cannot make the change itself (and in that sense, it does not usurp the other branches' functions), the jury can provide feedback to these other branches so that they will take action. Admittedly, nullification is an inexact form of signalling. It is most effective when jury after jury nullifies to express disagreement with a particular law or with the way in which a particular law is being enforced. When there is a pattern of nullification, as there was during Prohibition, then it is easier for the other branches to discern the message and to respond.

According to this view, then, the jury is not usurping the legislature's or executive's respective functions; rather, it is merely signalling to these other branches when they need to take action. For example, when the legislature passes a statute, the statute is necessarily written in general terms. When a jury nullifies, it is able to fill in the gaps, and to decide whether the statute was meant to cover the situation before it. When a prosecutor (the executive) chooses to enforce a statute in a certain way, he or she believes that such enforcement reflects the will of the populace. However, even if people support a statute in theory, they might think it should be enforced more narrowly in practice. A nullifying jury provides that feedback to the executive.

For example, in the case of the so-called "three strikes" law in California, under which those convicted of a serious felony after two prior felony convictions defined as "violent" or "serious" face a mandatory sentence of twenty-five years to life imprisonment,[86] enforcement eventually varied based on geography. In Northern California, where juries nullified and acquitted when they sensed that a case was a three-strikes case, prosecutors became more selective in which cases they chose to bring as three-strikes cases.[87] In contrast, in Southern California, and in particular in San Diego, where juries' convictions indicated greater support for the three-strikes legislation, prosecutors brought three-strikes cases more readily.[88] Although one criticism of nullification, as this example makes clear, is that it results in variation in a law that is supposed to be

---

86. *See* CAL. PENAL CODE § 667 (West Supp. 1998). The statute took effect on March 7, 1994, which was the date on which the Governor signed Bill No. 971. There was also a ballot initiative (Proposition 184), which was approved by voters on November 8, 1994, and took effect the next day, codified as CAL. PENAL CODE § 1170.12 (West Supp. 1998). The two statutes differ only in minor ways.

87. *See, e.g.,* Tony Perry & Maura Dolan, *Two Counties at Opposite Poles of "3 Strikes" Debate Crime: San Francisco Is Restrictive in Applying Law, San Diego Takes Hard Line, Approaches Reflect Will of Electorate,* L.A. TIMES, June 24, 1996, at A1.

88. *Id.*

applied uniformly, one benefit is that the law is being adjusted to meet the needs and norms of a geographical area.

Nullification and the Jury's Broad Role. Another benefit of nullification is that it gives jurors the opportunity to act in a manner consistent with their sense of what justice requires. The traditional view defines the jury's role narrowly: The jury is supposed to find facts and apply the law. This limited conception means that the jury will sometimes have to render a verdict with which it does not agree, but that it feels constrained to return by virtue of a narrow definition of its role.

The jury in *Inside the Jury Room* confronted this dilemma. The statute that Leroy Reed had allegedly violated had three criteria that had to be met. The prosecutor had to show that Reed was a convicted felon, that he possessed a firearm, and that he possessed it knowingly. According to the prosecutor, if the jury found that these three criteria had been met, then it had to return a verdict of guilty. Most of the jurors agreed that under a literal reading of the statute, they would have to return a verdict of guilty. However, they resisted a literal reading as too narrow in scope. They parsed the language of the statute, and found ambiguities. When some of the jurors were not altogether satisfied that the statute's language was open to alternative interpretations, they looked to their broader role as jurors. As one juror explained, if their role were as narrow as the prosecutor delineated, then there would be no need for a jury; a computer could do the job.

Instead, most of the jurors saw their role more broadly; they believed that they had been summoned as jurors in order to render a verdict that accorded with their sense of justice.

The jury struggled with how to define their role; not all of the jurors shared the same conception. One juror, a fireman, argued for a more literal interpretation of the statute and a more limited conception of the jury's role. He believed that if the three criteria of the statute were met, then they had no choice but to convict. He also saw the jury's role as limited to finding facts, applying the law, and nothing more. However, the other jurors ultimately persuaded him to change his vote, though it was unclear whether he actually changed his conception of the jury's proper role. With his capitulation, however, the jury agreed unanimously to acquit. The jurors did so, not because they thought they had ignored the law, but rather, because they thought they had acted consistent with a broader conception of their role, which required them to do justice.

Thus, nullification provides an outlet for the jury. It allows jurors to return a verdict that comports with their sense of justice. Without this outlet, jurors would, in some cases, feel that they had acted against their own better judgment. Certainly, it would be ironic if jurors, who are valued for the common-sense judgment that they bring to the decision-making process, were not allowed to exercise their own common-sense judgment. Jury duty is already difficult enough. It requires ordinary citizens to disrupt their everyday lives, to respond to a summons to serve in an official capacity as a juror, to observe a trial, to engage in often anguished deliberations, and ultimately, to render a judgment that "deal[s] pain and death."[89] Without nullification as a possibility, jury service would in some cases become even more difficult than it already is.

Of course, if every case resulted in a nullifying jury, the system would collapse. Nullification provides a useful safety valve if it is exercised only in dire circumstances—after the jury has struggled in its deliberations and can find no other way to do justice in the particular case. Professor Zeisel's observations about the hung jury are no less true of the nullifying jury.[90] Both play an invaluable role in the system, but both need to be exercised only when no other outcome is feasible.

The process by which a jury becomes a nullifying jury also is important. My own view is that there is a distinction between the jury or juror that is intent upon nullifying from the get-go and one that reaches that point of view only after careful and considered deliberation with fellow jurors. In the former case, the juror who begins jury service with a fixed mind is obviously not impartial and is in violation of his or her oath. John Grisham portrays this type of juror, albeit an extreme version, in *The Runaway Jury*. In the movie, this juror has a deeply-held desire to punish the gun companies because of the

89. Robert M. Cover, *Violence and the Word*, 95 YALE L.J. 1601, 1609 (1986).

90. *See supra* text accompanying notes 64–65.

death of his girlfriend in a shooting incident at school. This juror actively searches for a gun case in which to put his plan into effect, even if it means manipulating his background information so that he will not be removed peremptorily or for cause. Because it is a legal thriller, this juror goes on to commit far more egregious violations of the jury system, including contact with the parties and a bidding war to exact the highest price from the party willing to pay to have the case decided in its favor.

Grisham's fictional juror, who is intent upon ignoring the law in pursuit of his own personal agenda, stands in stark contrast to the jury in *Inside the Jury Room*. The Wisconsin jury begins its deliberation by having each juror express his or her views, which at this stage are quite tentative. The more the jurors deliberate, the more they question. They begin with a literal interpretation of the statute, but find such an approach too mechanical. They move on to examine any ambiguities in the language of the statute. Some find that there is room in the language of the statute to allow them to decide this case in a just manner, whereas others look to the broader role of the jury to arrive at justice.

Although the result may appear to be the same for the Wisconsin jury as it is for the Grisham juror—in that both jury and juror have chosen not to follow the law—the process each uses to reach that result is quite different. The Wisconsin jurors began as impartial jurors without a fixed view of the case; when they took their oath they meant it. They did not deceive the court, as did the Grisham juror. The Wisconsin jurors deliberated in good faith. They struggled in their deliberations and finally reached a result that they thought was consistent with the larger purposes of the jury. In this sense, then, they engaged in a law-regarding process, as opposed to the Grisham juror who epitomized a law-defying process.

The Policy Issue: Should Courts Instruct Juries on Nullification?

Courts believe that juries have the *power*, but not the *right*, to nullify. Juries have this power because they conduct their deliberations in secret. The basis for a jury's verdict (whether based on nullification or not) remains known only to those inside the jury room. Courts reason that secrecy during deliberations serves a number of important functions,[91] and is worth preserving even if it gives juries the opportunity to nullify. Courts have concluded, however, that because juries do not have a right to nullify, they should not receive any instruction on nullification. No federal or state courts instruct on nullification.[92] However, several recent outside efforts to

[91]. *See* United States v. Thomas, 116 F.3d 606, 608 (2d Cir. 1997) (discussing the functions served by secrecy during jury deliberations).

[92]. The federal circuits do not allow an instruction on nullification. *See* Marder, *supra* note 85, at 310 n.116 (listing cases). Only two states, Indiana and Maryland, permit judges to instruct jurors that they have the right to determine the law as well as the facts, *see id.*, but the two states' judiciaries have narrowed this right through case law. *Id.* (providing cases).

educate jurors about nullification should lead courts to reconsider whether to instruct jurors on nullification, not as a matter of law, but as a matter of policy.

Recent Efforts To Publicize Nullification. Courts, by opting not to instruct juries on nullification, have created a void into which special-interest groups and individuals have stepped. These special-interest groups and individuals are often willing to undermine respect for the jury and the court because its serves their organizational goals. Although their immediate goal is to inform jurors about nullification, they do so because they regard the jury as a vehicle for challenging laws with which they disagree.

For example, the Fully Informed Jury Association (FIJA), a libertarian organization consisting of members who oppose a panoply of laws, including drug laws, gun laws, and motorcycle-helmet laws, has tried several different approaches. One approach has entailed FIJA members standing on the courthouse steps and distributing leaflets to prospective jurors about to enter. These leaflets inform prospective jurors about their power to nullify and warn them that the court will not instruct them on this power, and might even go so far as to instruct them that they do not have this power. The leaflet invites prospective jurors to exercise this power, particularly in cases involving any of the laws to which FIJA members are opposed. In addition, the leaflet suggests other sources of information about nullification, including FIJA's Web site, telephone hotline (1-800-tel-jury), bumper stickers, newsletter, and catalogue merchandise.

A second approach that FIJA has taken is to initiate referenda that would require state courts to inform jurors of their power to nullify. FIJA recently supported such a referendum in South Dakota. If successful, the referendum would have required South Dakota state courts to inform juries of their power to nullify. The referendum would have allowed defendants "to argue the merits, validity and applicability of the law, including the sentencing laws."[93] Although the measure garnered some support, it was ultimately defeated.[94] Not surprisingly, prosecutors, judges, and many lawyers opposed the initiative.

A third approach that FIJA has taken is to lobby state legislators in a number of states to propose legislation that would inform jurors of their power to nullify. Although this approach has not led to the passage of any legislation thus far, it has attracted supporters along the way. For example, between 1991 and 1996, bills appeared in twenty-five state legislatures that would require judges to instruct juries that they had the power to judge the law as well as the facts.[95]

93. Adam Liptak, *A State Weighs Allowing Juries To Judge Laws*, N.Y. TIMES, Sept. 22, 2002, at A1.

94. *See, e.g.*, Bernard McGhee, *Four Ballot Issues Decided by Voters*, A.P. NEWSWIRES, Nov. 6, 2002 ("With all of the precincts reporting, Constitutional Amendment A had 68,622 votes in favor, or 22 percent, and 245,046 votes against it, or 78 percent.").

95. Joe Lambe, *Bill Would Let Juries Decide Law in Cases: Legal Establishment Reacts to Measure with Shock, Dread*, KAN. CITY STAR, Apr. 8, 1996, at A1.

Paul Butler, a former prosecutor in Washington, D.C. and now a professor at George Washington Law School, has proposed another grass-roots effort to inform jurors of their power to nullify. His approach varies from that of FIJA's in that he has focused on informing African-American jurors of their power to nullify. He does not worry about the myriad ways in which his proposal will harm the jury; rather, his focus is on the African-American community. His hope is that African-American jurors will choose to nullify in cases involving nonviolent, victimless crimes (i.e., drug cases) in which African Americans are defendants.[96] His view is that African-American jurors should use this little-known power of nullification in order to acquit African-American defendants in certain criminal cases. He views race-based nullification as a means of protesting the criminal justice system's racist treatment of African Americans and as a means of thwarting a system intent upon sending African-American men to prison rather than allowing them to remain in their communities where they are sorely needed.[97] Although he has suggested grass-roots methods to reach African-American jurors with his message, such as through word-of-mouth and local churches, thus far, his proposal has appeared in a journal[98] and magazines[99] likely to reach

96. *See* Butler, *supra* note 56, at 677.

97. *Id.* at 691.

98. *See id.* at 677.

99. *See* Paul Butler, *Black Jurors: Right to Acquit? (Jury Nullification)*, HARPER'S MAG., Dec. 1, 1995, at 11 (carrying an

a more limited readership than FIJA's grass-roots campaign.

If some jurors are learning about nullification, whether from FIJA's leaflets, South Dakota's referendum, or Butler's articles, the question is whether courts should instruct all jurors so that they enter the jury room equally well-informed about nullification. Courts can no longer assume that all jurors have no knowledge of nullification. Now that some jurors have some information (whether accurate or not), the question is whether courts should step in and ensure that all jurors are educated about nullification in language that the court chooses and through an instruction that courts, rather than legislatures, have carefully crafted. My own view is that courts should step in, but there are strongly held views on both sides of the debate.

Drawbacks of a Court Instruction. Many judges are reluctant to instruct jurors on nullification because they want to limit jury nullification. Although judges are not of one mind on the sub-

abridged version of Butler's *Yale Law Journal* article); *see also* Jeffrey Rosen, *Journey to Justice*, NEW REPUBLIC, Dec. 9, 1996, at 27 (book reviews) ("Accepting the idea of legal instrumentalism—that blacks should use power, when they have it, to serve the interests of the black community—Butler called on African American jurors to use their power to free guilty black defendants accused of nonviolent drug crimes.").

ject,[100] the prevailing view is that if jurors do not know about nullification, then they are less likely to engage in it. This view holds that even if jurors are not told about nullification, they will arrive at the concept (though they might be unfamiliar with the legal term) because they can think of no other way to do justice in their case. They will realize that they can nullify even without having been instructed on nullification. Thus, they do not need to be told because they will arrive at the answer for themselves. Moreover, if they had been told, then they might engage in nullification too readily, particularly when there might have been other ways to resolve the case without resorting to nullification.

Judges also worry that if they instruct jurors on nullification, this puts an undue burden on jurors. Jurors would then feel that it was their responsibility not only to apply the law, but also to judge the law. Moreover, this would cause a greater blurring in the respective roles of judge and jury, and of legislature and jury, than already exists. Judges have described a nullifying jury as one that is acting more like a mini-legislature than a jury. They worry about twelve jurors substituting their judgment for

100. *See, e.g.,* United States v. Dougherty, 473 F.2d 1113 (D.C. Cir. 1972) (writing for the majority, Judge Leventhal provided reasons against an instruction on nullification, and writing in dissent, Judge Bazelon offered reasons in support of such an instruction).

that of a majority of legislators. They also worry that jurors may start to feel as if they should "represent" a constituency or particular point of view, much the way that legislators do, rather than that they should vote as individuals guided by their own sense of judgment.

Finally, judges resist an instruction because they do not want to authorize the jury to act in a way that they regard as lawless. Judges take an oath to uphold the law, just as jurors do. Judges expect jurors to abide by their oath, just as judges do. Anything less is a threat to the rule of law and the legal system. From a judge's perspective, then, there is something almost perverse about having to tell jurors that they can nullify—that they can choose not to follow the law. Although judges may not always be able to stop juries from nullifying, at the very least, they feel that they should not have to assist juries to nullify.

Justifications for a Court Instruction. One of the most compelling reasons for judges to instruct the jury on nullification is that it allows the court to be candid with the jury. The jury has the power to nullify, and it should be told that it has this power. To do anything less is to reveal a certain distrust of the jury.

Judges who believe that the court ought to instruct jurors on nullification worry that without such an instruction, jurors might enter the jury room with different, and perhaps conflicting, information. Those jurors who had fortuitously received a FIJA leaflet on the courthouse steps, for example, would know about nullification, whereas those who had not would remain uninformed. The latter jurors would not know whether juries had such a power. They would not know whether to believe their fellow jurors with the FIJA leaflet who said that they did, or the judge, who has suggested, by defining their role so narrowly, that they did not. Later, when they discovered that the jury did in fact have such a power, they might feel that the court had deceived them. Or, even if they did not reach that level of distrust, they might nonetheless resent that they had had to struggle with whether they had the power (as did the Wisconsin jury in *Inside the Jury Room*) when the court could have easily given them that information so that they could have focused their attention on the verdict itself.

Another reason for the court to instruct on nullification is that if all the jurors have this information, then they might be able to prevent those who are of a mind to abuse nullification from doing so. Those who attempt to nullify based on improper motive, such as prejudice, could be questioned, challenged, and perhaps even stopped. Without knowledge about nullification, however, it becomes more difficult for jurors to challenge each other and to insist that they act from good motives.

Although it is true that jurors can learn of nullification from other sources, such as movies, books, and magazine articles, why leave such important information to the vagaries of chance? Why not ensure that all jurors enter the jury room with a basic understanding of nullification just as the court introduces jurors to other legal concepts that they will need to perform their job?

In some state courts, attorneys are permitted to tell jurors about nullification, sometimes directly and sometimes obliquely. But even if lawyers can allude to nullification, it is not the same as when this information comes from the court. Lawyers are advocates, and jurors know to take what they say with a grain of salt. If a juror is to trust what he or she hears about nullification, then it needs to come from the court.

At bottom, the two approaches to a nullification instruction reveal two different levels of trust of the jury. The judge who resists a nullification instruction expresses a certain distrust of the jury. He or she believes that it is better to withhold the information for fear of what the jury might do with it. In contrast, the judge who is willing to instruct on nullification trusts the jury and wants the relationship between judge and jury to be marked by candor rather than deception. This judge is willing to inform the jury about its power to nullify out of the belief that all jurors should have access to this information, and that they will use it carefully and advisedly. Indeed, the two positions do not have to be that far apart. A judge could instruct in language that advises jurors of the nullification power, but counsels them to use it with great restraint and only in those rare cases where justice truly requires it.

CHAPTER 9

POSTVERDICT ISSUES

The deliberations are a key stage for the jury, yet little is known about them except as revealed through postverdict interviews with jurors. The jury reveals little about its deliberations through official mechanisms. Once the jury has reached a verdict, the foreperson sends a note to the judge indicating as much. The jury returns to the courtroom, as do the parties. In the presence of the judge, parties, and public, the foreperson reads the verdict aloud. In a criminal case, the foreperson announces whether the jury has found the defendant guilty or not guilty; in a civil case, the foreperson announces whether the jury has found the defendant liable or not liable. In a criminal case, the judge typically polls the jurors individually to make sure that they are in accord with the verdict.[1] Once this has been done, the judge thanks the jurors for their service and dismisses them. At this point, the jurors are free to leave.

Although practices vary from courtroom to courtroom, some judges interview the jurors after they have been dismissed; they might allow the attorneys to do so as well. When jurors who have served in a

1. *See* FED. R. CRIM. P. 31(d) (Poll of Jury).

high-profile case leave the courthouse, the press also tries to interview them. Through these various postverdict interviews, judges, attorneys, journalists, and the public can begin to learn about the jury's experience in general and the jury's deliberations in particular.

Postverdict Juror Interviews

Postverdict Interviews with the Judge

Some judges have adopted the practice of speaking to jurors informally after jurors have completed their jury service. There are several reasons for a judge to do this. One reason is that it allows the judge to reassure jurors that they have done a good job and that the court appreciates their work. Jury service is not easy. Jurors are asked to make difficult decisions that have serious consequences. They have no special training for the job. When a judge meets with jurors after the verdict, the judge can reassure the jurors that they have done all that was expected of them and the judge can thank them again for their service. A second reason is that the judge can answer general questions that jurors still have as long as they do not pertain to the verdict the jury reached. It allows the court to tie up "loose ends" that still may trouble jurors. A third reason is that the judge can learn from jurors about their jury experience, and in particular, whether there are any steps the court can take to improve the experience for jurors in the future. In the course of this interview, judges are unlikely to ask jurors about their deliberations unless one of the jurors or attorneys raises a question of juror misconduct.

Some judges use this postverdict exchange with jurors as an opportunity to have them complete a questionnaire in which the jurors comment on their experience. The jurors' responses to the questionnaire provide a judge with a picture over time of what jurors liked about their jury service, what they disliked about it, and how the experience can be improved.

Postverdict Interviews with the Attorneys

In some courtrooms, jurors also have the opportunity to meet informally with the attorneys after the trial. This exchange can benefit jurors and attorneys alike. Attorneys often want to know what jurors thought of the case. They want any feedback that the jurors can provide. After watching the attorneys throughout the trial, jurors usually have views on what they did or did not like about the attorneys' approaches and many are happy to share their views with the attorneys. Such feedback can help the attorneys in their preparation in future cases.

Attorneys also are interested in the deliberations. They want to know which arguments were persuasive, which witnesses were credible, and which points the jury thought were important. Of course, there is also the risk that attorneys will use these interviews to probe more deeply than they should about the deliberations. Attorneys are not permitted to inquire into the reasoning of the jurors during the deliberations; this is protected by the secrecy in which the deliberations were conducted. There is a thin line, however, that separates permissible from impermissible lines of inquiry, and this is usually left to the attorneys and jurors to navigate. Although attorneys also will be interested in whether there was any juror misconduct, this concept is narrowly defined, at least in federal court. In federal court, juror misconduct is limited to whether any juror introduced any "extraneous prejudicial information" into the jury room during the deliberations or whether any juror was subject to "any outside influence."[2]

In one federal jurisdiction, attorneys are not permitted to interview jurors after the the verdict without permission of the court.[3] Another jurisdiction discourages such interviews.[4] One federal circuit denied an attorney's request to interview jurors after the verdict on the grounds that a defendant's right to a fair trial and a juror's right to privacy overcome a lawyer's right to free speech.[5] One rea-

2. *See* FED. R. EVID. 606(b).

3. *See, e.g.,* CONN. FED. LOC. CT. R. 12(f)(1) ("No juror shall respond to *any* inquiry as to the deliberations or vote of the jury or of any other individual juror, except on leave of Court....") (emphasis added).

4. *See, e.g.,* 1 WIS. CIV. JURY INSTRUCTION COMM., WISCONSIN JURY INSTRUCTIONS (CIVIL) 197 (1994) ("While nothing prohibits you from disclosing what happened in the jury room, you do not have to discuss the case with anyone or answer any questions about it.").

5. *See* Haeberle v. Texas Int'l Airlines, 739 F.2d 1019, 1021–22 (5th Cir. 1984).

son to discourage such interviews is that an attorney's questions at this stage could appear to the juror as a violation of his or her privacy. The juror has performed his or her public service and now wants to return to private life as quickly as possible. The juror may view additional questions as an intrusion, particularly because at this stage he or she is no longer "a juror." Another reason to prohibit attorney questions is that they appear to violate the secrecy of the jury deliberations. The comments made during the deliberations are protected by jury room secrecy and jurors should not be pressured into divulging them. Yet another reason is that attorneys can abuse the opportunity. There is a danger that they will use the interview as a fishing expedition to learn whatever they can about the deliberations. In those jurisdictions in which postverdict interviews with attorneys are prohibited or in which there are certain limitations, the judge typically advises the jurors of these restrictions before dismissing them.

Postverdict Interviews with the Press

Perhaps the most controversial postverdict interviews are juror interviews with the press. These interviews do not arise in ordinary, run-of-the-mill cases because such cases do not typically generate outside interest. However, these interviews do arise in high-profile cases. In such cases, members of the press seek out jurors because they believe that their readers or viewers will be interested in what the jurors have to say about the case.

Seeking Interviews. In high-profile cases, as in other cases, once the judge dismisses the jurors, the jurors are free to leave the courtroom. They have completed their service as jurors and can resume their lives as private citizens. In high-profile cases, however, jurors often encounter the press as they descend the courthouse steps (unless they are lucky enough to find a side exit by which to leave). Members of the press are eager to interview jurors in a high-profile case, and sometimes, it is a two-way street. Some jurors are eager to be interviewed; they want to give their account of what occurred in the jury room. However, other jurors do not want to talk to the press, or to anybody else, about what took place in the jury room. They might have found the deliberations difficult, and they have no desire to recount it or to relive it. They now find themselves thrust into the limelight, even though they do not want to be there. Even in the refuge of their homes, they are inundated with phone calls, including requests for interviews, television shows, and even book contracts. In one high-profile case, a juror who was pursued by the press finally fled to a Caribbean island in order to escape from the myriad requests and the unrelenting publicity,[6] and another who felt "[h]e was being hounded" simply chose

6. David E. Rosenbaum, *Prayer Was the Turning Point, a Juror Says*, N.Y. TIMES, May 5, 1989, at A19 (citing the experience of Juror Tara Leigh King).

to "disappear" for awhile.[7]

Why These Interviews Should Give Pause.
Although press interviews in high-profile cases have
become fairly commonplace, they nevertheless raise
some questions that should give pause. One such
question is whether the press's persistence leaves
jurors feeling "hounded." After performing their
jury service, especially in a case that they might
have found difficult, and after deliberations that
they might have found tense, jurors must contend
with being in the limelight and talking about an
experience that some want to put behind them. In
general, there are no rules that govern how the
press should behave toward jurors after a trial. If
the members of the press want to pursue jurors,
they are free to do so. If they want to keep jurors in
the spotlight, they are free to do that as well. This
territory is uncharted and an almost "Wild West"
attitude prevails. The press can pursue jurors as
vigorously as they choose (within the bounds of the
law); jurors are left to their own devices if they
want to avoid further interviews.

In addition to the question whether jurors feel
hounded by the press and the related question
whether the press's pursuit of jurors is unseemly,
these interviews raise several other questions that
have not yet been addressed by most courts. One
question is whether courts should offer any guidance or protection to jurors, particularly because
they were summoned by courts to perform this very

7. James Feron, *Jurors in Harris Trial Re-enacted Night of
Murder Deliberations*, N.Y. TIMES, Feb. 26, 1981, at A1.

public role. Do courts have an obligation to step in and to assist jurors because they did not volunteer for the role of juror? A related question is whether courts should issue any general caveats about interviews with the press. Some jurors have no qualms about being interviewed and discussing the deliberations. One difficulty with their perspective, however, is that they might seek to portray themselves in the best possible light. Thus, their comments may be plentiful, but unreliable. Those jurors who are portrayed poorly by the publicity-seeking jurors might think it unseemly to respond. Do courts have any obligations to educate the public about the ways in which juror accounts can be distorted, particularly when the press, which relies on such accounts to make their stories interesting, is unlikely to do so?

Another question is whether those jurors who reveal to the press what they or other jurors have said during deliberations violate the secrecy of the deliberations. Although jurors on a petit jury do not swear to keep the proceedings secret, as grand jurors do,[8] nevertheless, many jurors might think that comments made during deliberations are protected by the secrecy of the deliberations. Do those jurors feel deceived by the court or their fellow jurors when they see their deliberation comments on the front page of the newspaper? Eventually, this leakage could have a chilling effect on the deliberations. If juror comments can be revealed

---

8. *See* Fed. R. Crim. P. 6(e) (Recording and Disclosure of Proceedings).

through postverdict interviews, will future jurors be more circumspect in their comments during deliberations and will the candor of the deliberations suffer?

A Shift in Values. One reason for courts' restrained approach is that after a verdict there is a shift in the values at stake. During a criminal trial, for example, courts ensure that the defendant's Sixth Amendment rights to a fair trial and an impartial jury are protected.[9] Although there is still a First Amendment[10] right of the press to be present at the trial and to keep the public informed, this right is weighed against the defendant's Sixth Amendment rights, and courts usually err on the side of protecting the defendant's Sixth Amendment rights during the trial.[11] In spite of the press's right to cover the trial, they are not allowed to compromise the fairness of the trial or the impartiality of the jury. For example, federal courts, though they have experimented with cameras in the courtroom,

9. The Sixth Amendment provides in relevant part: "In all criminal prosecutions, the accused shall enjoy the right to a speedy and public trial, by an impartial jury of the State and district wherein the crime shall have been committed...." U.S. CONST. amend. VI, § 1.

10. The First Amendment provides in relevant part: "Congress shall make no law ... abridging the freedom of speech, or of the press...." U.S. CONST. amend. I.

11. *See, e.g.,* Nebraska Press Ass'n v. Stuart, 427 U.S. 539, 560 (1976) ("It is not asking too much to suggest that those who exercise First Amendment rights in newspapers or broadcasting enterprises direct some effort to protect the rights of an accused to a fair trial by unbiased jurors."); Sheppard v. Maxwell, 384 U.S. 333, 362, 355 (1966) (reversing the denial of habeas on the

have, for the most part, rejected the practice.[12] Federal judges worry that cameras compromise a defendant's right to a fair trial and detract from the serious purpose at hand. However, many state courts permit cameras in the courtroom.[13]

Once the trial is over, however, the First Amendment right of the press to report on the trial and to keep the public informed takes center-stage, and there is no competing Sixth Amendment right of the defendant at this point. Jurors might have a competing right of privacy, but it usually gives way in light of the press's First Amendment right to report on the trial and the public's right to be informed. Moreover, what jurors have to say about the trial could be viewed as precisely the kind of important political speech that the First Amendment was meant to protect. There will be some jurors who want to speak out, and some members of the public who want to hear their speech, and thus, courts appear hard-pressed to constrain either.

Even if jurors are shy of the press and want only to return to their private lives, there is an argu-

ground that petitioner was denied his right to "receive a trial by an impartial jury free from outside influences" when "bedlam reigned at the courthouse during the trial and newsmen took over practically the entire courtroom, hounding most of the participants in the trial").

12. *See, e.g.,* Bruce D. Brown, *Cameras Roll into Federal Court Again,* LEGAL TIMES, May 6, 1996, at 14.

13. *See, e.g.,* Todd Piccus, Note, *Demystifying the Least Understood Branch: Opening the Supreme Court to Broadcast Media,* 71 TEX. L. REV. 1053, 1064 (1993) (explaining that "forty-seven states permit broadcast coverage of at least part of their court system").

ment that they have played a public role as jurors and that they should be held accountable for the way they performed that role. According to this view, the press plays a vital role in revealing what went on during jury deliberations. The view is that jurors might act more responsibly during deliberations if they know that what they say will be subject to public scrutiny after the verdict.

However, a countervailing argument is that jury duty is already difficult enough and most jurors take their task quite seriously and perform it quite ably.[14] If jurors are subject to second-guessing by those who were not at the trial and not present during the deliberations, then the role of juror will become that much more onerous and the task of securing future jurors that much more challenging.[15]

Steps Courts Can Take. Rather than leaving jurors to fend for themselves with press interviews, courts should take steps to exercise some control over the process. There is a range of alternatives available to courts. At one end of the spectrum,

14. A National Law Journal poll of nearly 800 people who had served as jurors in civil and criminal cases nationwide in 1992 indicated that "jurors generally gave themselves high marks" and thought they "understood their mission and performed it well." Joan M. Cheever & Joanne Nalman, *The View from the Jury Box*, NAT'L L.J., Feb. 22, 1993, at S2.

15. *See* BOATRIGHT, *supra* note 40 (Ch. 5), at ix-x (identifying several reasons why citizens are failing to answer their jury summons).

courts could instruct jurors that they are not to speak to anybody, including the press. Federal judges in Connecticut currently do this.[16] Connecticut federal district court judges instruct jurors as follows: "No juror shall respond to any inquiry as to the deliberations or vote of the jury or of any other individual juror, except on leave of Court...."[17] One justification for this approach is that it protects the secrecy of the deliberations.[18] When jurors in federal court in Connecticut enter the jury room and deliberate, their comments will not go beyond the walls of that jury room. Another justification is that it respects the privacy of the jurors. At a time when jurors are fearful for their safety and protective of their privacy, the practice assures them that Connecticut federal courts have taken steps to protect both.

Some state courts have taken a middle ground. In these states, judges instruct jurors before dismissing them that they can talk to whomever they want,

16. *See* CONN. FED. LOC. CT. R. 12(f)(1).

17. *Id.*

18. *See* Abraham S. Goldstein, *Jury Secrecy and the Media: The Problem of Postverdict Interviews*, 1993 U. ILL. L. REV. 295, 310 (recommending passage of a statute "making it a crime for anyone without court permission to seek information from jurors about their deliberations, or for jurors to provide such information").

but that they should not feel compelled to do so; the decision is an individual one. Armed with this information, jurors know their rights. They know that when a microphone is thrust in their face, they need not agree to be interviewed; they can "just say no." A number of states, including Colorado, Idaho, Texas, and Wisconsin, have opted for this approach.[19] Federal courts in Kansas, Louisiana, Oklahoma, and Wyoming have taken a similar approach.[20]

At the other end of the spectrum, there are states that leave jurors to their own devices. They do not

19. *See, e.g.,* 1 COLO. SUPREME COURT COMM. ON CIV. JURY INSTRUCTIONS, COLORADO JURY INSTRUCTIONS 3D, § 1:16, at 37 (1988) ("It is now proper for you to talk to anyone, including the attorneys and parties, about this case. Whether you do so is entirely up to you."); IDAHO PATTERN JURY INSTRUCTION COMM., IDAHO JURY INSTRUCTIONS—CIVIL 145 (1988) ("For your guidance, the Court instructs you that whether you talk to the attorneys, or to anyone else, is entirely your own decision."); TEX. R. CIV. P. 226a, at 78 ("[After your discharge] ... [y]ou will then be free to discuss the case and your deliberations with anyone. However, you are also free to decline to discuss the case and your deliberations if you wish."); 1 WIS. CIV. JURY INSTRUCTION COMM., WISCONSIN JURY INSTRUCTIONS (CIVIL) 197 (1994) ("While nothing prohibits you from disclosing what happened in the jury room, you do not have to discuss the case with anyone or answer any questions about it.").

20. *See* KAN. FED. LOC. CT. R. 123(a)(9) ("No juror has any obligation to speak to any person about any case and may refuse all interviews or comments."); LA. FED. LOC. CT. R. (M.D., W.D.) 13.05 (same); OKLA. FED. LOC. CT. R. 47.2 ("Upon the discharge from service, each juror is free to discuss, or refuse to discuss, said juror's service with any person if the juror so desires."); WYO. FED. LOC. CT. R. 309(b) ("No juror has any obligation to speak to any person about any case and may refuse all interviews and comments.").

restrict jurors' postverdict interviews in any way and they do not inform jurors about their options with respect to postverdict interviews. In such jurisdictions, it is simply each man for himself.

Experimental Approaches That Courts Have Tried. Some judges have experimented with restricting jurors' postverdict interviews with the press based on time or scope. These judges have attempted to balance the need to protect jurors after the trial with the need to allow the press to perform its job, as guaranteed by the First Amendment. By imposing limited restrictions, these judges have attempted to strike a proper balance between the two competing needs.

In *United States v. Doherty*,[21] the district court judge restricted the press from seeking interviews with jurors for a week following the verdict. The case involved multiple defendants charged with various counts of conspiracy to commit mail fraud, perjury, and violations of the Racketeer Influenced and Corrupt Organizations Act (RICO).[22] During the course of the trial, the jurors were sequestered and their names and addresses withheld. After the jury rendered its verdict, the jurors met with the judge and expressed their desire not to have their names and home addresses released. The newspapers wanted the court to make this information available to them immediately while the public was still interested in the case. The judge sought to accommodate the competing interests: the jurors'

21. 675 F.Supp. 719, 723–24 (D. Mass. 1987).

22. 18 U.S.C. §§ 1961–1968.

interest in protecting their privacy and the press's commitment to informing the public. The judge ruled that for one week, jurors' names and addresses would not be disclosed and the press was not to interview the jurors. The judge agreed, however, to lift his order after a week, by which point the jurors would have had a chance to reflect on their jury experience and to decide how much of it they wanted to share with the press.

In another case, *United States v. Cleveland*,[23] upheld on appeal,[24] the trial judge restricted juror interviews with the press based not on time but on scope. After a well-publicized trial involving high-profile government figures charged with racketeering and related offenses, the jury found some of the defendants guilty and some not guilty. After the verdict, the judge instructed the jury as follows: "[A]bsent a special order by me, no juror may be interviewed by anyone concerning the deliberations of the jury."[25] Several newspapers challenged this order as a violation of their First Amendment right to gather news. The judge explained that the order was narrowly tailored to apply only to jury deliberations, that the case involved well-known defendants with power and influence, and that the court needed to keep the deliberations confidential to keep the jurors free from harassment and to protect free speech within the jury room in future cases.[26]

23. 1997 WL 412466 (E.D. La. 1997) (Vance, D.J.).

24. 128 F.3d 267 (5th Cir. 1997).

25. 1997 WL 412466, at *4.

26. *Id.* at *16.

The Fifth Circuit affirmed the district court judge's order, noting that although the restriction was not limited in time, it was limited in scope.[27] Unlike some past restrictions, which the Fifth Circuit had found overly broad,[28] this restriction was limited just to the jurors (and did not include their "relatives, friends, or associates") and was limited to their deliberations (and did not include their general reactions to the case).[29] Moreover, the Fifth Circuit explained, while the press must have access to what is available to the general public, the First Amendment does not give it any special access to that which is inaccessible to the public-at-large, such as jury deliberations.

Other Postverdict Issues Pertaining to Jurors

There are several other issues that can arise for jurors in the postverdict phase. Some of the issues, like juror misconduct, will arise infrequently. Other issues, such as appellate review of the jury verdict, will arise often and should be explained to the jurors so that they understand that it is part of the judicial process.

Juror Misconduct

One issue that can arise is juror misconduct. Juror misconduct can occur during the trial or deliberations, but may not come to light until after the verdict. Juror misconduct that occurs during

27. 128 F.3d at 269.

28. *See, e.g.*, United States v. Harrelson, 713 F.2d 1114 (5th Cir. 1983); *In re* The Express-News Corp., 695 F.2d 807 (5th Cir. 1982).

29. *In re* The Express-News Corp., 695 F.2d at 808.

the trial can be more visible to the judge and others, whereas juror misconduct that arises during the deliberations is harder to discern. When the latter is raised after the verdict, the judge has an obligation to interview the jurors and to see whether there has, in fact, been juror misconduct.

In federal court, juror misconduct that comes to light after a verdict has already been reached is limited to narrow circumstances. The *Federal Rules of Evidence* err on the side of insulating jury deliberations from outside scrutiny. Juror misconduct is limited to the juror who introduced extraneous prejudicial information to the other jurors or who was subjected to outside influence.[30] Even when such claims are made, they rarely succeed.[31] The judge is not permitted to inquire into the juror's reasoning or "mental processes" during deliberations.[32] Although the standard for juror misconduct in federal court is narrow, state courts are free to develop their own standards.

There are not many instances of juror misconduct because jurors try to perform their job responsibly and because courts are reluctant to probe too deeply into jury deliberations; however, there are some instances. For example, in one New York State civil case, *Lam v. Cheng*, an action for defamation and intentional infliction of emotional harm, the jury found in a 5–1 vote that there was not defamation by some of the defendants, that there was defama-

30. *See* FED. R. EVID. 606(b).

31. *See* Marder, *supra* note 5 (Ch. 8), at 496 n.182.

32. FED. R. EVID. 606(b).

tion by one defendant but not with reckless disregard of the statement's falsity, and that the one defendant who had made such a statement with reckless disregard had not caused harm to the plaintiff's reputation or standing in the community.[33]

After the verdict, the jury foreman, a white man, testified that he had been verbally abused by four jurors—three African-American women and one Latina. He claimed that the four jurors expressed racial hostility toward him throughout the deliberations, accused him of having a homosexual encounter with the plaintiff's lawyer in the courthouse bathroom, and derided him for reporting their racist statements to the judge. Another juror, an African-American man, agreed with the foreman's account of the racial animus expressed during the deliberations. The four jurors had accused the African-American juror of being an "Uncle Tom" when he did not agree with their view of the evidence. The four jurors continued to express their racial animus toward the foreman and the juror who disagreed with them, in spite of the judge's admonitions that race should play no part in the deliberations.

The court, after observing that jury verdicts should only be disturbed in exceptional circumstances, found such circumstances in this case. The racial prejudice of the four jurors impugned the

33. *See Jury Verdict Is Rejected as "Irrational," "Tainted by Racial Animus"; Lam v. Cheng*, N.Y.L.J., Sept. 10, 2001, at 25.

jury's ability to assess the evidence impartially. The court said that the affidavits of the two jurors, as well as their earlier complaints to the judge of racist behavior in the jury room, were not mere after-thoughts raised by disaffected jurors but attested to bias by the four jurors and that such bias constituted juror misconduct. The court set aside the verdict, which it found irrational and motivated by racial animus and pressure, and granted plaintiff's motion for a new trial based on juror misconduct.

Juror Stress

Another issue that can arise in particularly diffi-cult, lengthy, or emotionally draining cases is ju-rors' postverdict stress. Although there have always been such cases, courts seem more aware today of their effects on jurors and the court's need to pro-vide some assistance. Courts have begun to experi-ment with providing a psychologist, psychiatrist, or social worker for jurors to talk to after they have completed their jury service.[34] For example, after the Jeffrey Dahmer case, in which Dahmer had been charged with the murder of a number of young boys, and jurors had been subjected to testimony about cannibalism and sex with corpses, the trial judge advised jurors after the verdict that two psy-chiatrists would be made available to them. This would give them the opportunity to "talk, cry or vent rage."[35]

34. *See* JURY TRIAL INNOVATIONS, *supra* note 22 (Ch. 5), at 203–05.

35. Dirk Johnson, *Dahmer Jurors Tell of Emotional Impact*, N.Y. TIMES, Feb. 17, 1992, at A11.

Trial Judge's Review of Jury Verdicts and Awards

As important as the jury verdict is, it is still subject to further review by the trial judge (except when there is an acquittal in a criminal case), and, ultimately, to review by the appellate court. The judge should explain these different levels of review to the jury after it has reached its verdict.

After the jury verdict, whether in a civil or criminal case, the losing party can file a motion asking the judge to review the verdict. In a civil case, the party asks the judge to render a judgment as a matter of law.[36] In other words, the party argues that the judge should grant the motion because there was "no legally sufficient evidentiary basis for a reasonable jury" to find for the other party on that issue.[37] In a criminal case, the party asks the judge to render a motion for judgment of acquittal.[38] In the criminal context, the defendant argues that the government's evidence was "insufficient to sustain a conviction."[39] In both contexts, these motions can be made before the case is submitted to the jury and then also renewed after the jury has returned a verdict.

In civil cases, the judge can review not only the jury's verdict, but also its damage award. Through

36. *See* FED. R. CIV. P. 50(b). This motion can be made before the case goes to the jury, as well as after the jury reaches a verdict.

37. FED. R. CIV. P. 50(a) (Judgment as a Matter of Law).

38. *See* FED. R. CRIM. P. 29(c). Like its counterpart in the civil context, this motion can be made before the case has been submitted to the jury.

39. FED. R. CRIM. P. 29(a).

remittitur[40] and *additur*,[41] the judge can decide whether to decrease or increase the amount that the jury has awarded to the winning party. In other words, the jury's damage award is not the final word. Even though press coverage of damage awards, particularly large awards, often focuses on the jury's award, the judge also has a role to play in this process.[42] Often the judge will reduce the damage award for reasons the jury could not have been aware of, such as the need to adhere to a state statute that mandates a cap on damage awards for noneconomic injury, such as pain and suffering. Thus, the judge's reduction of the jury's damage award does not necessarily signal that the jury "got it wrong," but rather, that the jury was not given all of the information to which the judge was privy. Hence, the judge should explain to the jury that the award of damages is a two-step process that involves both jury and judge. Otherwise, jurors might simply feel that their work was unnecessary.[43]

40. Remittitur is "the power to reduce damages" and is recognized "by virtually all judicial systems." JACK H. FRIEDEN-THAL, ET AL., CIVIL PROCEDURE § 12.4, at 560 (2d ed. 1993).

41. Additur is "the power to increase damages" and "has not been accepted in all courts," *id.*, largely because it did not exist under common law. This led the Supreme Court to hold in *Dimick v. Schiedt*, 293 U.S. 474 (1935), that it violated the Seventh Amendment. *Id.* However, some state courts have upheld its constitutionality under state law. *See* FRIEDENTHAL ET AL., *supra* note 40, at 561.

42. *See* Marder, *supra* note 37 (Ch. 3), at 429, 437–39; Neil Vidmar et al., *Jury Awards for Medical Malpractice and Post-Verdict Adjustments of Those Awards*, 48 DEPAUL L. REV. 265, 298–99 (1999).

43. *See, e.g.*, Mark Curriden, *Jury Awards Fall Under Weight of Obscure Law; Sometimes, Jurors' Desire To Mete Out Justice*

Juries and Sentencing in Criminal Cases

In a criminal case, the judge also sentences the defendant if there has been a conviction. With the exception of capital sentencing schemes in some states, where juries are asked in a separate penalty phase of the trial to recommend either the death penalty or a life sentence,[44] the jury has not traditionally played a role in sentencing. In both federal and state courts, that task has been left to the judge, who, at least in federal court, must sentence in accordance with the *United States Sentencing Guidelines*.[45] In practice, however, the prosecutor plays a significant role under the *Sentencing Guidelines*. The prosecutor's decision about which charges to bring against the defendant will, in many cases, determine the sentence because, under determinate sentencing schemes, such as the *Sentencing Guidelines*, very little discretion is left to the judge. Although juries in some states used to play a role in sentencing, that has not been the practice throughout most of our history.[46]

Is Outweighed by State's Limits on Amounts, DALLAS MORNING NEWS, May 7, 2000, at 1A (quoting a juror who felt that the jury's struggle to award punitive damages was unnecessary, given the trial judge's decision to reduce the award afterward due to a statutory cap).

44. *See, e.g.*, Marder, *supra* note 15 (Ch. 3), at 891 n.62 (listing some of the states that have juries play a role in sentencing in capital cases, such as Arkansas, Florida, Mississippi, New Mexico, Oklahoma, and Oregon).

45. U.S. SENTENCING GUIDELINES MANUAL (1998) [hereinafter SENTENCING GUIDELINES].

46. *See* Nancy J. King, *The Origins of Felony Jury Sentencing in the United States*, 78 CHI.-KENT L. REV. 937 (2003).

In several recent Supreme Court decisions, however, the Court has begun to articulate a new, more expansive role for jury fact-finding, so that it now extends to sentencing. This new role was announced in *Apprendi v. United States*,[47] applied to a death penalty case in *Ring v. Arizona*,[48] to a state sentencing procedure in *Blakely v. Washington*,[49] and will soon be applied to the *Sentencing Guidelines* in *United States v. Booker*.[50]

In *Apprendi*,[51] the Supreme Court addressed the question whether the Due Process Clause of the Fourteenth Amendment required that a jury make a factual finding beyond a reasonable doubt before the maximum prison sentence for an offense punishable by ten years could be made punishable by twenty years. Apprendi pleaded guilty to two counts (a second-degree offense of possession of a firearm for an unlawful purpose and a third-degree offense of possession of an antipersonnel bomb) of a 23–count indictment charging him with various shootings. After the plea agreement, the prosecutor dismissed the remaining counts against him, except for a count seeking an enhancement of the sentence based on biased purpose; Apprendi reserved his right to challenge the hate crime sentence enhancement on constitutional grounds. The second-degree

47. 530 U.S. 466 (2000).

48. 536 U.S. 584 (2002).

49. ___ U.S. ___, 124 S.Ct. 2531, 159 L.Ed.2d 403 (2004).

50. United States v. Booker, ___ U.S. ___, 125 S.Ct. 11, 159 L.Ed.2d 838 (2004) (granting the petition for writ of certiorari).

51. 530 U.S. at 469.

offense carried a penalty of five to ten years and the third-degree offense carried a penalty of three to five years. After an evidentiary hearing on Apprendi's " 'purpose' " for the shootings, the judge concluded that the crime " 'was motivated by racial bias' " and held that the hate crime enhancement applied.[52] The judge sentenced Apprendi to a twelve-year term of imprisonment for the hate crime, and to shorter concurrent sentences on the other two counts.

Apprendi argued that the Due Process Clause required a jury, rather than a judge, to have made the factual finding beyond a reasonable doubt that his crime was motivated by racial bias before his sentence could be lengthened beyond the statutory maximum for the possession charges. The Court agreed with Apprendi. The Court held that the state practice in which a defendant is convicted of a second-degree offense based on a finding beyond all reasonable doubt, but then is punished based on a separate proceeding in which a judge finds by a preponderance of the evidence that the defendant's purpose was to " 'intimidate,' " could not stand.[53] The Court looked to the history of the jury, and the protections it afforded a defendant, and concluded that the State's practice circumvented these protections. Apprendi was entitled to have a jury find beyond a reasonable doubt every element of the crime with which he was charged. Labelling the alleged bias a "sentencing factor" rather than an

52. *Id.* at 471.
53. *Id.* at 491.

element of the offense did not obviate the need for a jury finding beyond a reasonable doubt.

In *Ring v. Arizona*,[54] the Supreme Court extended *Apprendi* to the capital context, and in so doing, overruled an earlier case, *Walton v. Arizona*.[55] In *Ring*, the Court concluded that defendants who faced a death sentence, just like those who faced a life sentence, were entitled to "a jury determination of any fact on which the legislature conditions an increase in their maximum punishment."[56]

Timothy Ring was convicted by a jury of felony murder occurring in the course of armed robbery. The evidence presented at trial failed to prove beyond a reasonable doubt that he was a major participant in the robbery or that he had actually fired the shot that killed the guard. Under Arizona law, he could not be sentenced to death unless there were additional findings. State law permitted the judge to sentence the defendant to death only if there is at least one aggravating circumstance and it is not outweighed by mitigating circumstances. During the sentencing hearing, the judge went on to make additional findings, including that Ring was a major participant and was the one who shot the guard. In addition, the judge determined that there were two aggravating factors and that they outweighed the mitigating circumstance; the judge sentenced Ring to death.

54. 536 U.S. 584 (2002).

55. 497 U.S. 639 (1990).

56. 536 U.S. at 589.

Ring argued that Arizona's sentencing scheme allowed the judge to make findings of fact that increased his penalty, and that this violated the Sixth and Fourteenth Amendments to the U.S. Constitution, which required that such findings be made by a jury. The Supreme Court agreed. The logic of *Apprendi* required such a conclusion. In *Ring*, the Court returned to its understanding of *Apprendi* that if "a State makes an increase in a defendant's authorized punishment contingent on the finding of a fact, that fact ... must be found by a jury beyond a reasonable doubt."[57] *Apprendi* provided this protection to defendants facing a life sentence; *Ring* held that this protection applied no less to defendants facing a death sentence. In reaching this result, the Court reversed an earlier decision, *Walton v. Arizona.*[58] The Court explained in *Ring* that *Walton* was irreconcilable with *Apprendi* because *Walton* had upheld Arizona's sentencing scheme, which allowed a judge to find aggravating factors necessary for imposition of the death penalty that had not been found by a jury[59] and this scheme was no longer constitutional after *Apprendi*.

In *Blakely v. Washington*,[60] the Court held unconstitutional a state sentencing procedure in which the judge assigned a sentence beyond the prescribed statutory maximum without the jury having found

57. 536 U.S. at 602 (citing Apprendi v. New Jersey, 530 U.S. 466, 482–83 (2000)).

58. 497 U.S. 639 (1990).

59. 536 U.S. at 609.

60. ___ U.S. ___, 124 S.Ct. 2531, 159 L.Ed.2d 403 (2004).

the facts required to establish the additional time. Mr. Blakely, who pleaded guilty to the kidnaping of his estranged wife, had agreed to facts that supported a maximum sentence of fifty-three months. However, the court made a judicial finding that Mr. Blakely had acted with " 'deliberate cruelty,' " and therefore, it imposed an "exceptional" sentence of ninety months.[61] Mr. Blakely argued that the judge, by making these findings, had violated his Sixth Amendment right to a jury trial because the facts that would support the additional thirty-seven months in prison had neither been admitted by Mr. Blakely nor found by a jury.

Although *Blakely* only applied to a state sentencing procedure, it raises a serious question about the constitutionality of the *Sentencing Guidelines* as currently applied. The *Sentencing Guidelines* have been applied without requiring the jury to make certain factual findings. The Supreme Court recently agreed to hear two cases, consolidated for oral argument, that will allow it to address some of the consequences of *Blakely* for the *Sentencing Guidelines*.[62] This line of sentencing cases, in which the jury's fact-finding function is required for sentencing purposes, provides one way in which the U.S. Supreme Court is broadening the jury's role in the criminal context.

Appellate Review of Verdicts and Damage Awards

Just as the jury does not have the final word on the verdict or the damage award, the trial judge

61. *Id.* at 2535 (quoting state statute).

62. *See supra* note 50.

does not have the final word either. After the jury has rendered its verdict and award, and the judge has acted on any motions for judgment as a matter of law (civil) or judgment of acquittal (criminal) as well as motions to decrease or increase the damage award (civil) or for a new trial (both civil and criminal), the losing party can appeal from the final judgment as a matter of right, meaning that the appellate court has to hear the case; its review is not discretionary.

Although the jury verdict and award in a civil case are subject to review by the appellate court, the standard that the appellate court uses is highly deferential to the jury. The appellate court applies a deferential standard to any factual findings the jury might have made, as indicated in a special verdict[63] or interrogatories.[64] The appellate court will accept these findings unless they are "clearly erroneous." The appellate court is less deferential toward the trial judge's legal conclusions and instructions, which can be reviewed "de novo." One reason for the difference in standards is that the appellate court can judge the law from the record below and is in as good a position as the trial judge, if not better due to its distance from the trial proceedings, to render a judgment as to the correct law. However, it is much harder for an appellate court to put itself in the position of a jury that has sat through a trial and made certain credibility determinations in

63. *See* FED. R. CIV. P. 49(a) (Special Verdicts).

64. *See* FED. R. CIV. P. 49(b) (General Verdict Accompanied by Answer to Interrogatories).

the course of its deliberations in order to reach certain factual findings as a jury. Therefore, although the jury's factual findings are subject to review by trial and appellate judges, they are reviewed according to a deferential standard.

In a criminal case, the jury returns a general verdict of either guilty or not guilty. If the latter, then there is no further review by an appellate court; the jury's verdict is final. If the former, the appellate court can review it, but because it is a general verdict,[65] there are no factual findings on the record. Thus, in a criminal case, a defendant can ask the appellate court to review the trial judge's instructions and rulings on the law. As in the civil context, the appellate court is in as good a position as the trial judge, if not better, to decide the law, and thus, the standard of review is de novo.

Postverdict Update of Jurors

After jury trials in both civil and criminal cases, judges need to explain to jurors what can happen to their verdict or their damage award as the trial judge and then the appellate court review it. If jurors are given such information, even if it is only a thumbnail sketch, they will have a better understanding of the work they have just done and of how it fits into the broader judicial process. For example, one judge uses postverdict letters to inform jurors about the progress of the case for which

65. *See, e.g.,* United States v. Spock, 416 F.2d 165 (1st Cir. 1969) (reversing a conviction of conspiracy to counsel draft evasion because the trial court had put to the jury ten special questions in addition to a general verdict).

they served as jurors.[66] In a criminal case, such an update might include the sentence the judge imposed. In a civil case, such an update can include whether the judge granted any motions. Just as trial judges might want to know what happened to their cases on appeal, jurors might want to know what happened to their cases upon sentencing or review of the verdict or damage award. This is a way of treating jurors with respect and appreciation, as well as contributing to their education about the role of the jury in the judicial process.

66. *See* Donald E. Shelton, New Jury System Ideas, Jury Summit 2001, N.Y., N.Y. (Feb. 3, 2001). I thank Judge Shelton for telling me about this practice that he has instituted in his courtroom.

Chapter 10

Current Criticisms of
the Jury System

There are several current criticisms of the jury system that have received a fair amount of attention in the popular press and in some state legislatures. In the civil context, the most resounding criticism is that jury damage awards are excessively high. Another criticism is that juries do not understand cases that are technical or complex. In the criminal context, juries have exposed racial tensions, which have led to the criticism, particularly in some high-profile cases, that jurors are motivated by racial solidarity or bias rather than evidence. To whites, this has meant that African-American jurors are failing to deliberate and to convict African-American defendants; to African-Americans, this has meant that white jurors convict when the defendant is African American. Although these are current criticisms, and will change over time, my goal here is simply to flag the issues and to raise questions about some of the quick-fix solutions that have been proposed and sometimes even adopted.

Excessive Jury Damage Awards in Civil Cases

One of the current criticisms of the jury system is that civil juries have run amok in awarding damages. These damage awards are the focus of criticism most often in products liability and medical malpractice cases. As a result of the high damage awards in medical malpractice cases, for example, doctors and insurance companies claim that juries have driven up the cost of malpractice insurance premiums. The increase in premiums has driven some doctors from the practice of medicine, which, in turn, has left some areas of the country with an inadequate number of doctors in particular specialties, such as obstetrics and gynecology. Some doctors are so angry about the situation that they have staged demonstrations and even work slowdowns.[1]

Legislators in both state and federal government have tried to respond to the doctors' and insurance companies' claims. In some states, legislatures have passed statutes limiting jury damage awards for noneconomic injury, such as pain and suffering.[2] In states that have taken this approach, a typical cap is $250,000. In other states, legislatures have passed

1. *See, e.g.*, Richard Lezin Jones & Robert Hanley, *Trenton Seeks a Compromise for Doctors*, N.Y. TIMES, Feb. 5, 2003, at B5 (describing a work slowdown by New Jersey doctors to protest the rising cost of medical malpractice insurance and to urge the state legislature to cap jury damage awards at $250,000 for pain and suffering in medical malpractice cases).

2. *See, e.g.*, Thomas Koenig & Michael Rustad, *His and Her Tort Reform: Gender Injustice in Disguise*, 70 WASH. L. REV. 1, 79 (1995) ("Twenty-one states have enacted some reform measure limiting non-economic damages in health care litigation.... [T]ort reformers have succeeded in capping non-economic damages in medical malpractice cases in several states.") (footnote omitted). Among the states that have passed statutes limiting pain and suffering awards in medical malpractice suits are Michigan, Wisconsin, and Utah. *Id.* at 79 n.331.

statutes limiting the types of cases that can be heard by a jury.[3] For example, in West Virginia, cases of infant injuries at birth are now heard by a judge rather than a jury.[4]

On the federal level, the issue has been the subject of much congressional debate. Although Republicans and Democrats in Congress do not agree on a reform, they do seem to agree that there is "a medical liability crisis."[5] In 2003, the U.S. House of Representatives passed a bill that would have imposed a cap of $250,000 on pain and suffering awards in medical malpractice cases; however, the Senate declined to consider the bill.[6] With the presidential election of 2004, the issue is back on the front page of newspapers because "President Bush has made jury award caps a central piece of his agenda for tort law changes."[7]

3. *See* Mark Curriden, *Tipping the Scales; Right to Trial by Jury Fades Under Court Rulings*, DALLAS MORNING NEWS, May 7, 2000, at 1A ("Forty-two states have restricted the types of cases that juries can hear.").

4. *See* Mark Curriden, *The Shrinking Role of Juries*, DALLAS MORNING NEWS, May 7, 2000, at 23A.

5. Senator Bill Frist, the Republican leader, has described the medical malpractice issue as " 'a national emergency that is hurting people.... It's a crisis that is increasing.' " Sheryl Gay Stolberg, *Senate Refuses to Consider Cap On Medical Malpractice Awards*, N.Y. TIMES, July 10, 2003, at A20 (quoting Senator Frist). According to another article, even "Democrats concede that there is a medical liability crisis." Sheryl Gay Stolberg & Carl Hulse, *Resigned to Failure, G.O.P. Still Pushes Forward on Malpractice Cap Bill*, N.Y. TIMES, July 8, 2003, at A18.

6. *See, e.g.*, Stolberg, *supra* note 5, at A20.

7. Stolberg & Hulse, *supra* note 5, at A18.

Although capping jury awards for noneconomic injuries is a popular reform, particularly among Republicans in the House of Representatives and the Executive, it is unclear that juries are the cause of the medical liability crisis. Indeed, insurance companies have not said that premiums would be lowered even if a national cap were imposed on jury awards for noneconomic injury. The insurance industry goes through cycles and the rise in premium costs is more likely due to the cyclical nature of the industry than to jury awards. Juries also seem an unlikely cause of rising premium costs, given how few cases actually go to trial and are heard by a jury.[8] Moreover, the patient who has been most seriously harmed by a negligent physician is the one who will lose the most with a cap. Although the cap is supposed to address the problems of frivolous lawsuits and excessive jury awards, it does neither. Rather, it affects the suits that are the least frivolous and it affects the damages that are the most deserved due to the extensive harm suffered by the patient.

If legislatures want to reduce jury awards, there are several steps that could be taken before limiting the jury by imposing a cap or taking the case away from the jury altogether, but it is unclear that reducing jury awards is even the right goal. There is scant evidence that "many" jury damage awards

8. *See* OWEN M. FISS & JUDITH RESNIK, ADJUDICATION AND ITS ALTERNATIVES: AN INTRODUCTION TO PROCEDURE 9, 19, 22 (2003) (noting that only 3% of all civil cases and 6% of all criminal cases went to trial in federal courts in 2000, and that the percentage of cases that went to jury trial was even smaller).

are "too" high. Although press coverage focuses on the high awards, it does so because they are of interest and make for dramatic stories, not because they are representative of most jury awards.[9] In fact, empirical studies suggest that the win-rate among plaintiffs in products liability and medical malpractice cases is low, and that when plaintiffs do win, the awards tend to be modest.[10] Furthermore, even when plaintiffs win and juries award them damages, the judge often reduces the damages through remittitur.[11]

If the problem is that jury damage awards are inconsistent, rather than too high, then there are

9. *See, e.g.*, Daniel S. Bailis & Robert J. MacCoun, *Estimating Liability Risks with the Media as Your Guide: A Content Analysis of Media Coverage of Tort Litigation*, 20 LAW & HUM. BEHAV. 419, 423–26 (1996) (studying newsmagazine coverage of tort litigation and finding that product liability and medical malpractice cases were overrepresented).

10. *See id.* at 419, 423–26; Deborah Jones Merritt & Kathryn Ann Barry, *Is the Tort System in Crisis? New Empirical Evidence*, 60 OHIO ST. L.J. 315 (1999) (analyzing data from Franklin County, Ohio, and finding that plaintiffs' win-rates in product liability and medical malpractice cases tended to be low, and when they did win, their awards were modest).

11. *See* William Glaberson, *Juries, Their Powers Under Siege, Find Their Role Is Being Eroded*, N.Y. TIMES, Mar. 2, 2001, at A1 (describing a study by Professors Kevin M. Clermont and Theodore Eisenberg, in which they found that federal appeals courts now reverse civil jury damage awards in injury and contract cases 40% of the time, as compared to 20% of the time in 1987). This proclivity to engage in remittitur is not limited to injury and contract cases. *See, e.g.*, Suja A. Thomas, *Re-examining the Constitutionality of Remittitur Under the Seventh Amendment*, 64 OHIO STATE L.J. 731, 745 (2003) (finding that judges reduce jury damage awards in many civil rights cases).

several steps that courts can take to ensure greater consistency, though it is unclear that inconsistency is even a problem. According to one empirical study, which analyzed data from verdict reporters in three states, juries reached consistent awards for pain and suffering in medical malpractice suits and the awards were not as high as press accounts suggested because they were often reduced by judges in the postverdict period.[12]

If inconsistency were the problem, however, juries could be given some guidance about an appropriate damages award. If judges gave jurors data about past awards in comparable cases, as at least one jury scholar has proposed, then they would have some benchmark or "guidepost" for deciding how much damages to award in the case before them.[13] This proposal also included a return to the twelve-person civil jury to reduce the variability of jury awards,[14] a proposal unlikely to garner much political support at a time when juries are under attack and when economic cutbacks are the order of the day. Yet another step to ensure greater consistency of jury damage awards would be to use special verdicts or interrogatories, which are procedural devices already available under the *Federal Rules of*

12. Vidmar et al., *supra* note 42 (Ch. 9), at 298–99.

13. *See* Diamond et al., *supra* note 37 (Ch. 3), at 317–18. Diamond's research built upon Peter Schuck's suggestion that courts provide juries with "schedules" so that they have some guidance as they struggle to determine damage awards. Peter H. Schuck, *Mapping the Debate on Jury Reform, in* Verdict: Assessing the Civil Jury System 306, 325–26 (Robert E. Litan ed., 1993).

14. *See* Diamond, *supra* note 37 (Ch. 3), at 318.

Civil Procedure.[15] By relying on these tools, judges could outline to the jury the way they should approach the issue of damages, just as they do now for some verdicts. Thus, there are incremental steps that courts could take and information courts could provide to assist juries in determining damage awards without legislatures simply wresting power away from juries to decide this issue.

Jury Incompetence in Technical and Complex Cases

The criticism that juries are incompetent to decide technical and complex cases has been made for some time. The argument is that because jurors are laypersons, there is no expectation that they have received any technical training. Therefore, it is unlikely that they can understand, much less decide, a case that involves technical or complex issues. They will not understand the vocabulary, concepts, exhibits, or the testimony of the expert witnesses.

As an illustration of this problem, consider Stephen Adler's description of the jury that heard the case in *Brooke Group Ltd. v. Brown & Williamson*,[16] in which the defendant tobacco company was alleged to have engaged in anticompetitive behavior in violation of the Robinson-Patman Act. In Adler's book,[17] each chapter focuses on a discrete jury trial

15. *See* FED. R. CIV. P. 49(a) & (b) (Special Verdicts and General Verdict Accompanied by Answer to Interrogatories).

16. Brooke Group Ltd. v. Brown & Williamson Tobacco Corp., 509 U.S. 209 (1993).

17. STEPHEN J. ADLER, THE JURY: TRIAL AND ERROR IN THE AMERICAN COURTROOM (1994).

and exemplifies a particular weakness in the jury system. In his chapter on jury incompetence,[18] Adler described a North Carolina jury that had to decide a complicated antitrust case. During the lengthy trial, the jury was presented with statistical analyses from expert witnesses, and yet most of the jurors had had limited business experience and education. (For example, none of the jurors had progressed beyond high school.) Adler suggested that the jurors were ill-equipped to understand, much less to critique, the testimony, particularly if the trial issues were not made more accessible to them by the judge and his instructions on the law. It was not surprising, according to Adler, that the U.S. Supreme Court eventually held that a reasonable jury could not have reached the verdict that this jury had.[19]

Those who criticize the civil jury for incompetence, especially in complex or technical cases, have advocated a number of solutions, ranging from specialized juries to substituting judges for juries. A specialized jury is one that would consist of laypersons who have had training in technical areas. Their jury service would not be limited to just one case. The idea is that they would have the requisite training to understand the issues, but they would still be ordinary citizens called to serve. One drawback, however, is that they could become hardened over time, just like some judges are said to be-

18. *Id.* at 116–44 ("What's a Blivet?").

19. 509 U.S. at 243.

come.[20] In contrast, under our current system, a juror serves for one case only and then returns to his or her private life. Another drawback is that the jury is supposed to bring the common-sense judgment of the community to bear on the issue at trial. A jury consisting of a narrow range of the population—those with training in technical areas such as science or engineering—will not have available to it as broad a range of perspectives as a jury that has been drawn from the population-at-large nor can it be said to represent the broader community's norms and judgment.

The Supreme Court recognized the limitations of a specialized jury in *Thiel v. Southern Pacific Co.*,[21] even though the specialized jury in that case was unintended. Thiel, who sued the railroad for not stopping him from jumping out of one of its trains and injuring himself when its agents knew that he was " 'out of his normal mind,' " challenged the jury panel because it consisted mostly of "business executives or those having the employer's viewpoint."[22] It turned out that the jury clerk and commissioner had adopted the practice of excluding daily wage earners from jury duty because of the economic hardship they thought it would impose on

20. *See* Duncan v. Louisiana, 391 U.S. 145, 156 (1968) ("If the defendant preferred the common-sense judgment of a jury to the more tutored but perhaps less sympathetic reaction of a single judge, he was to have it.").

21. 328 U.S. 217 (1946). For another discussion of this case in the context of a venire drawn from a cross-section of the community, see text accompanying notes 1–4 (Ch. 5).

22. 328 U.S. at 219.

such workers. The Supreme Court, however, recognized that daily wage earners might have an important perspective to contribute. A jury consisting of workers who were paid on a regular basis, just like a jury consisting only of those well-versed in technical matters, would "breathe life into any latent tendencies to establish the jury as the instrument of the economically and socially privileged. That we refuse to do."[23] The reasoning that led the Court to hold that the exclusion of daily wage earners violated the court's supervisory powers seems equally applicable to the creation of juries that consist only of the technically savvy.

Another proposal is to give technical or complex cases to judges rather than juries. One difficulty with this approach, however, is that the Seventh Amendment does not have a "complexity exception." To create one would be to rewrite the Seventh Amendment. Although the Seventh Amendment is not applicable to the states, and the states are free to structure their jury systems as they see fit, technical or complex cases require community judgments just as much as less complicated cases do. To exclude a whole body of cases from jury consideration (and who is to determine which cases are technical or complex?) would mean taking power away from juries and giving it to judges. These technical or complex cases can involve large sums of money and important competing values. These are precisely the kinds of cases that ought to be heard by juries.

23. *Id.* at 223–24.

My own view is that there is much that lawyers and judges can do to make even technical or complex cases accessible to jurors. Lawyers need to explain the issues in plain English, both to the judge and to the jurors. In addition, judges need to provide instructions in language that laypersons can understand. As discussed earlier,[24] there are many improvements that judges can make to their jury instructions: word choice, structure, and presentation can go a long way toward making the instructions more comprehensible.

In addition, courts need to be far more innovative in the tools that they give jurors in order to do their work, particularly in technical or complex cases. As discussed earlier, jurors should be given basic tools, like notepads and pens for note-taking[25] and calculators for determining damages. In complex cases in particular, the court should provide jurors with notebooks that contain such basic information as a list of the parties, lawyers, witnesses, copies of key exhibits, preliminary jury instructions, and a seating chart for the courtroom that identifies the trial participants.[26] The notebooks also should include legal terms of art that are likely to arise in the case. In complicated or lengthy cases, jurors would probably benefit enormously from the use of laptop computers. This one tool would allow jurors to take

24. *See supra* text accompanying notes 16–33 (Ch. 7) (discussing jury instructions).

25. *See supra* text accompanying notes 4–9 (Ch. 6) (discussing juror note-taking).

26. *See* JURY TRIAL INNOVATIONS, *supra* note 22 (Ch. 5), at 110 (suggesting contents of notebooks).

legible notes, to organize vast amounts of material presented at trial, and to have easy access to a juror notebook, the judge's instructions, a spreadsheet, and calculator, all of which could be downloaded at appropriate times. In sum, before cases are taken away from juries on the ground that they are too complex, every effort should be made to make them less complex. This effort should begin with the lawyers' arguments and the judge's instructions, but it should not end there; jurors also need the proper tools, including low-tech tools such as a juror notebook and high-tech tools such as a laptop computer.

The alternative to having a jury decide the case is having a judge decide the case, and judges are also vulnerable to the criticism that they do not understand technical cases. Indeed, District Court Judge Thomas Penfield Jackson, who heard the government's antitrust case against Microsoft, suggested that "his technology expertise was limited" and that he accepted the Justice Department's proposal to break up Microsoft because he thought that he could not " 'equip [himself] to do a better job than they [the Justice Department] have done.' "[27]

Some states, such as Michigan, are experimenting with the creation of specialized courts to hear technology and high-tech business cases. Michigan has created a court with judges dedicated to hearing technology cases who would receive special training

27. *See* Pam Belluck, *Michigan Plans a High-Tech Lure*, N.Y. TIMES, Feb. 22, 2001, at A10 (quoting Judge Thomas Penfield Jackson).

"to understand the complex issues that arise in technology disputes."[28] These judges would have the assistance of technological tools, such as video-conferencing, that will allow much of the court's business to be conducted in an efficient and convenient manner by parties accustomed to working with such tools. Through the use of videoconferencing and e-mail, the parties can be anywhere in the country when they present their case to the court.

The impetus for the creation of this "cybercourt" is that with such expertise and resources, parties will want to bring their disputes to this court and high-tech businesses will want to move to Michigan. Just as Delaware is a popular forum for corporate litigation, Michigan hopes to become a popular forum for technology litigation. It remains to be seen how this experiment will fare. At the very least, this experiment takes the "carrot" approach by offering parties a speedy and convenient resolution to their dispute, rather than the "stick" approach of depriving them of their right to a jury trial by mandating that such cases be heard by judges. In fact, Michigan's cybercourt will be limited to cases that do not require a jury, that involve sums of money greater than $25,000, and that have the agreement of both parties to use this court.[29]

Biased Jurors in Criminal Cases

One criticism in some criminal cases, particularly in high-profile criminal cases, is that jurors are

28. *Id.*

29. *Id.*

biased based on race. This criticism takes different forms, depending on the race of the defendant, the victim, the jurors, and the lawyers. This criticism is usually made in terms of juries consisting of black jurors and white jurors, but of course, juries are often far more racially diverse than the black/white dichotomy suggests.[30]

Many African Americans view the criminal justice system as biased against them. According to one law professor, Paul Butler, the criminal justice system is racist; it was designed by whites to oppress blacks.[31] According to Butler, blacks are ensnared by the criminal justice system and sent off to prison in numbers that are disproportionately high compared to their numbers in society.

Butler's suggestion to African Americans, given their minority status in society, is to use their power as jurors to acquit those African-American defendants charged with nonviolent, victimless crimes, such as drug violations. Some communities, such as Washington, D.C. and the Bronx, N.Y., with relatively large African-American populations, have been charged with an unusually high rate of acquittals,[32] perhaps taking Butler up on his suggestion.

30. *See, e.g.,* Nancy S. Marder, *Juries, Justice & Multiculturalism,* 75 S. CAL. L. REV. 659, 685 (2002) (conducting an empirical study of twenty-six criminal juries in Los Angeles in which the participating juries consisted, on average, of five Caucasians, three Latinos/as, two African Americans, and two Asian Americans).

31. *See* Butler, *supra* note 56 (Ch. 8), at 691.

32. *See, e.g.,* Benjamin A. Holden et al., *Color Blinded? Race Seems To Play an Increasing Role in Many Jury Verdicts,* WALL

Many African-American jurors, however, claim that they are not nullifying, as Butler has suggested, but rather, they are simply following the judge's instructions and voting to acquit because they have "reasonable doubt." They are less persuaded of the veracity of police testimony than white jurors because of how they have been treated by the police in their own communities. The jurors in the O.J. Simpson criminal trial explained that they acquitted because they had reasonable doubt.[33]

Whites' Criticisms of African-American Jurors

One criticism by some whites is that African-American jurors are failing to convict African-American defendants. Whether this is because they are flouting the law and nullifying (consistent with Butler's proposal) or because they have reasonable doubt (though they may require more work by the

St. J., Oct. 4, 1995, at A1 (claiming that in the Bronx, "black defendants are acquitted in felony cases 47.6 percent of the time—nearly three times the national acquittal rate of 17 per cent for all races"). *But see* Parloff, *supra* note 83 (Ch. 8), at 5, 6 (explaining that Bronx juries are not acquitting at unusually high rates, but are merely at the high end of the norm).

33. *See, e.g.*, Tony Knight, *Debating Simpson Verdict: Opinion Split on Whether Acquittal Was Really Condemnation of System*, L.A. DAILY NEWS, Oct. 16, 1995, at N1, *available in* 1995 WL 5422994 (" 'Things just didn't add up....' ") (quoting Juror No. 4, David Aldana); *Rivera Live: Analysis: Judging the Jury; How Commentators and the Public Feel Towards the Jurors in the O.J. Simpson Trial and the Trial of Christopher Lynn Johnson* (CNBC television broadcast, Oct. 20, 1995), *available in* 1995 WL 2735950 ("No one really thought [the evidence] was credible. You know, with Fuhrman, the collection of the evidence, the sock that had no blood then had blood—you know, these type of things.") (quoting Anise Aschenbach, Simpson juror).

prosecutor than white jurors require), they are perceived as acting out of racial solidarity with the defendant. One writer suggested, based on anecdotal rather than empirical evidence, that African-American women in particular fit this description.[34] His theory was that African-American women did not want to send more African-American men off to prison so they were failing to deliberate; he surmised that they were responsible for an increase in the number of hung juries.[35] However, an empirical study of hung jury rates in four parts of the country has not found any significant increase.[36]

Even though there has been no significant increase in the rate of jury acquittals[37] or hung juries,[38] some states have considered altering the jury's decision rule so that it is easier for juries to convict. Rather than require a unanimous verdict, as most states[39] and the federal courts require in a criminal trial,[40] some states have considered changing to a 10–2 or 11–1 decision rule. California, for example, debated such a change after the acquittal

34. *See* Rosen, *supra* note 56 (Ch. 8), at 54, 55.

35. *See id.*

36. *See* Hannaford-Agor et al., *supra* note 61 (Ch. 8), *available at* http://www.ncsconline.org.

37. *See* Parloff, *supra* note 83 (Ch. 8), at 6 (noting a national acquittal rate of about 28%). Parloff's figure would mean that about 72% of jury verdicts result in convictions or hung juries.

38. *See* Hannaford-Agor et al., *supra* note 61 (Ch. 8).

39. *See* Marder, *supra* note 15 (Ch. 3), at 945 n.308 (listing states that require a unanimous verdict in a criminal jury trial).

40. *See* FED. R. CRIM. P. 31(a) ("The verdict shall be unanimous.").

of O.J. Simpson in the state criminal trial.[41] Ironically, such a change in decision rule would not have affected the O.J. Simpson jury, which reached a unanimous verdict of not guilty.

The main drawback to this proposal is that all of the jurors would not have to listen to each other during the deliberations. They could simply enter the jury room, take a vote, and if they satisfied the new decision rule, they could return a verdict of guilty without ever having deliberated about the case. As discussed earlier,[42] the jury in *12 Angry Men* would have satisfied such a decision rule and would have convicted without any deliberation. Henry Fonda never would have had a chance to turn the jury around to his way of seeing the case. A change in the decision rule would have serious implications for the one or two jurors who disagreed with the other jurors. The other jurors would no longer feel the need to listen to them, persuade them, or challenge them; they could simply ignore them.

Another way to reduce the number of acquittals or hung juries is for the trial judge to excuse from the deliberations any juror who has announced his or her intention to nullify, assuming the jury has made the judge aware of such a juror. The issue arose in *United States v. Thomas*,[43] a criminal case in federal court in which several defendants were charged with violating the drug laws. Juror No. 5,

41. *See supra* text accompanying notes 53–55 (Ch. 8).

42. *See supra* text accompanying notes 37–39 (Ch. 8).

43. 116 F.3d 606 (2d Cir. 1997).

the only African-American juror on the jury, in a case in which all of the defendants were African Americans, tried to explain to both his fellow jurors, and eventually, to the judge that he had reasonable doubt and was unwilling to convict unless he could overcome his reasonable doubt.[44] It was unclear, however, whether his vote was based on racial solidarity[45] and could not be changed or whether it was based on reasonable doubt[46] and an understanding of the defendants' perspective that he could not communicate effectively to the other jurors. The other jurors sent a note to the judge advising him of their difficulty with this juror. After several interviews with this juror, as well as with the other jurors, the judge dismissed him from the jury, even though the jury was in the midst of its deliberations. The judge concluded that Juror No. 5 refused to convict based on " 'preconceived, fixed, cultural, economic, [or] social ... reasons that are totally improper and impermissible.' "[47]

On appeal, the Second Circuit tried to strike a balance between protecting the secrecy of the jury

44. During one of his interviews with the judge, Juror No. 5 explained: "When I make a decision to send someone to prison ... I want to know that it's clear in my mind beyond a reasonable doubt." Reporter's Transcript of Proceedings, Feb. 24, 1995, at 4029, United States v. Thomas, 894 F.Supp. 58 (N.D.N.Y. 1995).

45. When the judge interviewed the other jurors, one juror claimed that Juror No. 5 was voting for acquittal because the defendants were his " 'people.' " *Thomas*, 116 F.3d at 611.

46. Other jurors claimed that Juror No. 5 was basing his views on the evidence. *Id.*

47. *Id.* at 612 (quoting trial judge).

deliberations and having jurors follow the law and not nullify. The Second Circuit approved the practice of removing jurors who announced their intention to nullify, though in this case, the appellate court believed that the trial judge should have made a more searching inquiry into this particular juror's intentions.[48]

There are several drawbacks to the Second Circuit's approach. First, the judge exercises a supervisory role over the jurors during their deliberations once he is called in to assess a juror's intentions; it is unclear how this might affect the dynamics of the deliberations. Second, the judge has to second-guess that juror and decide whether he intends to nullify or whether he simply has reasonable doubt. The judge's interpretation of the juror's motivations may in turn be shaded by the judge's own view of the case. Having the judge exercise this supervisory role over the jury also might have a chilling effect on the jury's deliberations. The juror who has reasonable doubt and wants to vote to acquit may be pressured into changing his vote by fellow jurors who otherwise threaten to send a note to the judge. Even if the juror's vote is based on reasonable doubt, rather than nullification, he may change his vote to avoid an interview with the judge. Moreover, the juror who has such strongly held views, even if they are based on nullification, rather than reasonable doubt, should be allowed to act upon them, or at least this is my view, though admittedly it is a minority view.

48. *Id.* at 617–18.

African Americans' Criticism of White Jurors

Just as whites criticize African-American jurors for not seeing beyond race, African Americans criticize white jurors for not seeing beyond race, though in a different way. White criticism of African-American jurors is that they vote based on racial solidarity when the defendant is African American. African-American criticism of white jurors is that they vote based on racial animosity when the defendant or victim is African American.

One case that was, in many African Americans' view, an example of this phenomenon involved state criminal charges brought against white police officers Stacey Koon and Laurence Powell for the beating of African-American motorist Rodney King.[49] The beating was captured on videotape by an amateur photographer and replayed countless times on television channels throughout the country, as well as in the courtroom. In spite of the videotape, the largely white jury found the white police officers, Koon and Powell, not guilty. The not guilty verdicts sparked riots in Los Angeles and in several other cities around the country.

The white jurors explained that they had simply followed the judge's instructions on the law. They had parsed the instructions carefully and believed that they had followed them precisely.[50] For example, one juror explained that he felt constrained by

49. *See* People v. Powell, No. BA035498 (Cal. Super. Ct. L.A. County 1991); Richard A. Serrano, *All 4 Acquitted in King Beating*, L.A. TIMES, Apr. 30, 1992, at A1.

50. The jurors also could have been attempting to avoid responsibility for their decision. They could have been using a

the judge's instructions in the following way: " 'I believe there was excessive use of force, but under the law as it was explained to us we had to identify specific "hits" that would show specific use of force. It had to be beyond a reasonable doubt, and I just couldn't do that.' "[51] The jurors denied that they had acquitted Koon and Powell out of sympathy for them and enmity toward King or because they had engaged in nullification.

Many African Americans and whites were "shocked"[52] and "angered"[53] by the verdicts. They

close reading of the instructions as a way of justifying their view that the law compelled them to reach the decision that they reached. One commentator has noted this phenomenon in capital cases in which jurors believe that the law is compelling them to recommend a sentence of death so that they are absolved of responsibility. *See* William J. Bowers, *The Capital Jury: Is It Tilted Toward Death?*, 79 JUDICATURE 220, 223 (1996) (citation omitted).

51. Richard Lacayo, *Anatomy of an Acquittal*, TIME, May 11, 1992, at 30, 32.

52. *See, e.g.*, Leslie Berkman, *Verdict Shocks O.C. Chiefs, Black Leaders*, L.A. TIMES, Apr. 30, 1992, at A1 ("Shock and outrage were expressed by a number of Orange County police chiefs and leaders of the county's black community in the wake of the acquittal . . . ."); Serrano, *supra* note 49, at A1 (" 'I am shocked, outraged, and frightened for our nation . . . .' ") (quoting Dr. Joseph Lowery, President of the Southern Christian Leadership Conference); Ben Winton & Glen Creno, *Valley Blacks Angry, Frustrated, Say Justice Denied to Minorities*, ARIZ. REPUBLIC, Apr. 30, 1992, at A1, *available in* 1992 WL 8240037 ("Residents of Phoenix's white neighborhoods also were shocked by the verdict.").

53. *See, e.g.*, Larry Gross & Justin Blum, *4 Cops Found Not Guilty in Rodney King Beating*, CHI. DEFENDER, Apr. 30, 1992, at 1 ("Local residents and community leaders expressed anger, shock,

could not fathom how the jury had reached acquittals, except out of racial hostility toward the victim and racial connection to the defendants. The riots that followed the verdicts expressed the frustration and anger that African Americans felt with a criminal justice system that could produce such an outcome. Although the riots expressed the despair of many, and focused attention on juror bias, they did not offer a way of addressing it, if, indeed, bias was the explanation for the verdict.[54]

When Koon and Powell were tried by a diverse jury in a civil case in federal court in Los Angeles County for violating the civil rights of Rodney King, they were found liable. With a diverse jury, jurors are able to challenge each other's preconceptions more readily. "Groupthink,"[55] in which everyone agrees to what has already been said and is afraid to challenge the status quo, is less likely when jurors come from different backgrounds, experiences, and perspectives and are likely to bring these

outrage and disbelief Wednesday after a California jury found four white Los Angeles police officers not guilty in the beating of Black motorist Rodney King.").

54. Newspaper writers and commentators tried to help the public make sense of the verdicts, and in doing so, they offered several explanations: the jurors had become numb to the violence of the beating through repeated viewings of the videotape; the jurors tried to follow the instructions too closely, and missed the forest for the trees; or perhaps the jurors had engaged in jury nullification because they shared a similar background and outlook with the defendant police officers. *See* Marder, *supra* note 85 (Ch. 8), at 294–301 (providing a fuller discussion of explanations for the verdict).

55. IRVING L. JANIS, GROUPTHINK 7, 262, 270–71 (2d ed. 1982).

differences into the jury room and challenge each other's assumptions. Although there is no quick and simple way to mandate diverse petit juries without causing more harm than good, as the Supreme Court has long recognized,[56] there are a number of steps that will help to create diverse juries. These steps include: eliminating most exemptions, using multiple lists for the venire, updating those lists often, adopting a one-day one-trial requirement, and eliminating or reducing the number of peremptory challenges available to each side. As Justice Marshall noted in *Peters v. Kiff*,[57] diverse juries are needed not simply in cases in which race is explicitly discussed, but in all cases because we cannot foresee all of the subtle ways in which race comes into play in the courtroom.

Indeed, some researchers have found that in cases that deal explicitly with race, whites are more likely to recognize and resist their own stereotypical thinking than in cases with no mention of race, where they are less on their guard and more likely to engage in such thinking.[58] Thus, another way to

56. *See, e.g.*, Taylor v. Louisiana, 419 U.S. 522, 538 (1975) ("[W]e impose no requirement that petit juries actually chosen must mirror the community and reflect the various distinctive groups in the population."); Duren v. Missouri, 439 U.S. 357, 364 n.20 (1979) (noting that the fair cross-section "requirement does not mean 'that petit juries actually chosen must mirror the community'") (quoting *Taylor*, 419 U.S. at 538); Lockhart v. McCree, 476 U.S. 162, 173 (1986) (noting that petit juries are not required to "reflect the composition of the community at large").

57. 407 U.S. 493, 503–04 (1972).

58. *See* Samuel R. Sommers & Phoebe C. Ellsworth, *How Much Do We Really Know about Race and Juries? A Review of*

challenge juror bias, in addition to taking steps to create diverse juries, is to include voir dire questions about race in every case so that jurors are always on their guard against stereotypical thinking.[59]

Of course, voir dire is supposed to reveal prospective jurors' biases, but, as discussed earlier, the voir dire needs to be transformed in several ways if it is to accomplish this goal.[60] Prospective jurors need to be questioned about their attitudes and beliefs and they need to be questioned on an individual as well as a group basis. Racial bias poses a particular challenge during voir dire because, as prevalent as it is, most prospective jurors are loath to admit to it. When asked outright whether they can be impartial, they will say that they can be. Thus, it may be necessary to ask in more subtle ways and through different means (written and oral questioning) until contradictions emerge that suggest bias even if the prospective juror is unaware of or unwilling to acknowledge it.[61]

If anything positive can be said to have come from the trials of Koon, Powell and O.J. Simpson, it may be the importance of diverse juries, not just

Social Science Theory and Research, 78 CHI.-KENT L. REV. 997, 1029 (2003).

59. *Id.* at 1026–27.

60. *See supra* text accompanying notes 42–65 (Ch. 5).

61. *See* Neil Vidmar, *When All of Us Are Victims: Juror Prejudice and "Terrorist" Trials*, 78 CHI.-KENT L. REV. 1143, 1168–69 (2003) (noting inconsistent responses to a questionnaire in a high-profile case, suggesting that prospective jurors cannot always assess accurately their own impartiality).

because the contribution of a diverse group of people will lead to more ways of viewing a case and
perhaps to better decision-making, but also because
it will lead to greater community acceptance of the
verdict. The charge of juror bias was easy to make
in both the state criminal trial of Koon and Powell
and the state criminal trial of O.J. Simpson because
the former was a largely white jury and the latter
was a largely African-American jury. Juries that are
not diverse are more open to the charge of juror
bias, whether that is what motivated the jurors,
either subconsciously or self-consciously, in these
cases or not.

Although juries are far more diverse than they
have ever been, they still have a way to go. We have
progressed from the time when states could pass
statutes excluding African-American men from
serving on the jury, and when states could require
all women to register affirmatively before they were
allowed to serve as jurors. Only within the past
twenty years have courts made serious strides toward eliminating practices such as discriminatory
peremptory challenges that continued to keep African-American men and all women from actually
serving on juries even after the legal impediments
had been removed. However, we continue to live
with the repercussions of these earlier restrictions:
a deep and abiding suspicion that others are not
playing by the rules. White jurors worry that African-American jurors are acquitting or nullifying too
readily when the defendant is African American.
African-American jurors worry that white jurors are

motivated by racial animus when the defendant or victim is African American. The only way for citizens of all races to overcome these suspicions is by actually serving together on a jury. Even today there are few other settings in which people of different races, genders, classes, ages, and religions actually work together; the jury provides one of those rare settings.

CHAPTER 11

CONCLUSION

While the history of the jury, like the history of our country, has been marked by moments of distrust, the present time also holds out promise and reason for optimism. Juries are more diverse than they have ever been, and though they decide only a limited number of cases, the cases that they do decide are often of great importance.

The headlines are replete with jury trials that have captured national attention and that have significance, not just to the parties, but also to those outside the courtroom. For example, the jury verdicts in the criminal trials of Martha Stewart for perjury[1] and the Rigas family for defrauding Adelphia Communications,[2] are important both to the parties and to other heads of companies contemplat-

1. *See, e.g.,* Brooke A. Masters & Ben White, *Stewart Guilty on All Charges; Businesswoman Conspired with Broker, Jury Says,* WASH. POST, Mar. 6, 2004, at A1 ("Stewart's conviction was a major victory for the government in a series of corporate fraud cases brought after the collapse of the stock-market bubble and a wave of accounting scandals.").

2. *See, e.g.,* Barry Meier, *2 Guilty in Fraud at a Cable Giant,* N.Y. TIMES, July 9, 2004, at A1 (describing the case in which prosecutors charged the Rigases with using $2.3 billion in Adelphia funds for their own purposes and lying to investors and banks about the company's financial condition; the jury convicted the father and at least one son of conspiracy and fraud).

ing similar wrong-doing. One newspaper story described the Rigases' trial as "one of the most prominent in a wave of corporate scandals—WorldCom, Tyco International and ImClone Systems among them—that followed the collapse of Enron in 2001."[3] The juries in many of these cases sat for a long period of time and struggled with their verdicts. They performed an invaluable public service; they did the difficult work of trying to draw a line between acceptable and unacceptable behavior for company officials, and they did so at personal cost[4] and without personal gain.

Why Are Jurors Willing To Do This Job?

Admittedly, when most citizens receive their jury summons in the mail, they do not greet it with alacrity. Rather, they think about all the reasons they cannot serve and they come prepared with a list of excuses to tell the judge. However, a transformation occurs in the courtroom. Although prospective jurors begin jury service with their excuses in mind, unless the excuses are serious impediments to service, they soon fade. Ideally, jurors enter a solemn courtroom; they are introduced to the case by a dignified judge; and they begin the formal

3. *Id.*

4. Sometimes there was more personal cost than expected. Consider Juror #4 in the Tyco case. Members of the press thought that she had made a hand gesture, signalling "o.k." to the defendant, and focused attention on her and whether she was an impartial juror. She became the subject of so much press attention that ultimately her name was revealed and she received threatening letters. The trial judge eventually declared a mistrial in this case.

questioning of voir dire. At some point, perhaps through the process of voir dire, they are transformed from citizens who do not want to serve into citizens who are ready to serve.

Some explain this transformation in a cynical way, particularly in a high-profile case. They point to jurors as people who want their fifteen minutes of fame or who want the cash opportunities that could follow after serving in a high-profile case. However, most jury trials are not high-profile, and most jurors do not stand to gain anything from their service; in fact, most stand to lose because the juror pay of $5 to $40 per day rarely meets what a person would earn from his or her job.

I think the better explanation is the combination of civic responsibility and the power of the courtroom. Citizens undoubtedly respond to their summons out of a sense of civic obligation and adherence to the law, but it is the courtroom that helps persuade them that they really do want to serve. They are undoubtedly struck by the solemnity of the courtroom and the seriousness with which all who are present regard the proceedings. They see the parties before them and recognize that their participation as jurors will make a difference. Unlike an individual's vote in an election, one juror can actually change the outcome of a case. In addition, there is the human drama that every case potentially offers.

As a testament to the power of jury service, most jurors think more highly of the judicial system after

they have served than before.[5] They also believe
that their jury acted responsibly and did the best
job it could.[6] Indeed, most people remember their
jury duty years after they have served; they remember the case and how it was decided. Given the long-
lasting effects of jury service, and the way it can
shape jurors' views of the legal system, it behooves
us to make jury service as positive an experience as
possible.

What Can Be Done To Make the Job Less Onerous in the Future?

Although most jurors' experience in serving on a
jury is a positive one, there are steps that courts
can take to enhance the experience further. Technology has begun to play a role in improving jury
service, and it is likely to continue doing so in the
future.

Justice Brandeis wrote that states should serve as
laboratories,[7] and indeed, state courts are doing so
in introducing technology that will make jury ser-

5. *See, e.g.*, Stephanie Simon & Amy Dockser Marcus, *Jurors Don't Mind Duty, Survey Finds*, WALL ST. J., July 3, 1991, at B3 ("More than 80% [of jurors] said they came away with a favor- able view of their service, according to the survey of 8,468 jurors by the National Center for State Courts.").

6. *See, e.g., The Perfect Juror?*, NAT'L L.J., May 2, 1994, at A18 ("As shown in last year's National Law Journal poll of nearly 1,000 jurors, most of them take their jobs seriously and try to follow the law as best they can.").

7. New State Ice Co. v. Liebmann, 285 U.S. 262, 311 (1932) (Brandeis, J., dissenting) ("It is one of the happy incidents of the federal system that a single courageous State may, if its citizens choose, serve as a laboratory; and try novel social and economic experiments without risk to the rest of the country.").

vice more convenient and less daunting than it has been traditionally. Many state court systems have developed Web sites so that a citizen who is summoned for jury duty can take care of preliminary matters online. Prospective jurors can use court Web sites for matters both large and small: they can learn about the history and roles of the jury on the one hand, and where to park their car near the courthouse on the other.[8] They can seek postponements or excusals online, or check which day they will be needed without ever having to leave their homes. In some state court systems, they can even complete a preliminary questionnaire online so that the in-court voir dire can focus on matters specific to the case. Courts are just beginning to explore all of the ways that the Web can be used to make jury service less onerous.

Lawyers and judges are also beginning to experiment with ways to use technology in the courtroom so that their presentations are easier for jurors to understand. For example, some judges not only read the jury instructions aloud and give jurors a written copy to follow during the reading and to take with them into the jury room, but also videotape the reading of the instructions so that the jurors can replay parts as needed during the deliberations. In that way, jurors can return to the judge's reading and hear parts again, complete with the judge's intonations and emphases. Given that instructions

8. *See* Nancy S. Marder, *Juries and Technology: Equipping Jurors for the Twenty-First Century*, 66 BROOK. L. REV. 1257, 1272–73 (2001).

can sometimes last for hours and that instructions can be difficult to absorb like any lengthy lecture, this use of technology assists jurors to grasp the nuances after they have gotten the big picture.

Lawyers, too, are presenting their cases by using new technology. They can make an argument orally and also use Powerpoint to highlight their main points visually. They can use video presenters that allow them to show jurors an exhibit enlarged on a screen, with relevant parts highlighted or circled. All of the jurors can focus on the exhibit as it is being described, rather than the traditional way of passing the exhibit around from juror to juror, even as the lawyer has already moved onto the next point.

Of course, not all technology is helpful to jurors, and lawyers and judges need to proceed cautiously. Some jurors will be put off by technology; others will find themselves passively watching the presentation, as they would a television show or movie, rather than being actively engaged and carefully scrutinizing all that is said. In the move to replace traditional ways of presenting material, with new, more technologically sophisticated ways, lawyers and judges need to be careful that they do not lose jurors along way. They should present material in multiple ways, rather than simply replacing one format with another. Some jurors like having documents in front of them and being able to read them at their own pace; for such jurors, having the documents displayed on a large screen for a brief amount of time will not be an adequate substitute for holding and reading the actual document. However, young jurors, who are accustomed to getting information in brief snippets on the Internet rather than in lengthy articles in newspapers and newsmagazines, might appreciate a quick visual display. By branching out and presenting material in multiple forms, lawyers and judges might be more effective in reaching jurors who learn in different ways.

Finally, as courts and parties search for new ways to resolve disputes quickly and inexpensively, they have recognized that not all cases need to be heard by traditional juries sitting in traditional courtrooms. Just as judges in Michigan are experimenting with "cybercourts," where the parties can be anywhere in the country and use technology to reach the judges in Michigan,[9] others are beginning to experiment with "cyberjuries."[10] Cyberjuries rely on jurors who can hear a dispute presented to them in cyberspace. Although cyberjuries are still in a nascent stage, and still look more like opinion polls than deliberating juries, they have the potential to develop into a form of dispute resolution for some types of cases. With the development of new software, such as Unchat,[11] which allows a limited number of participants to engage in a deliberation facilitated by a group leader or foreperson, there is the possibility of group deliberation on the Web.

9. *See* Belluck, *supra* note 27 (Ch. 10), at A10.

10. *See, e.g.*, www.iCourthouse.com.

11. *See* Beth Simone Noveck, *Unchat: Democratic Solution for a Wired World*, *in* DEMOCRACY ONLINE: THE PROSPECTS FOR POLITICAL RENEWAL THROUGH THE INTERNET 21 (Peter M. Shane ed., 2004).

Although it is unlikely that cyberjuries will replace traditional juries any time soon, and there are some features—such as face-to-face deliberations—that cyberjuries might never replicate, these emerging forms of juries show the power of the traditional jury. The traditional jury remains both an evolving and inspiring institution. The traditional jury is evolving in the ways that it has incorporated new citizens and new technologies into this ancient institution. The traditional jury is inspiring in that new forms of juries are springing up using new technologies such as the Web. Although cyberjuries are no substitute for traditional juries, they have the potential to bring the jury experience to a much broader swath of the population than has been reached thus far. For example, they can reach those who are homebound, elderly, or primary caretakers and make some form of jury experience, albeit not identical to the in-court experience of the traditional jury, available to them. In that sense, then, these new forms of the jury reinvigorate the traditional jury and continue to make it a democratizing and vital force in our society.

Almost 170 years ago, Alexis de Tocqueville recognized that the jury played several broad roles in our society, far beyond its role as judicial administrator. Tocqueville described the jury as a "free school" teaching citizens about the responsibilities of self-governance in a democracy. He also recognized the jury's role as a "political institution," keeping governmental overreaching, whether by the executive, legislative, or judicial branches, in check.

The praise that Tocqueville had for the jury still rings true today. In fact, Tocqueville's observations have even greater resonance today when more of the citizenry can serve as jurors than was true in his time. The trust that Tocqueville had in the jury to play its different roles—deciding cases, educating citizens, preventing governmental overreaching by placing ordinary citizens in a position of responsibility—was not misplaced. The jury continues to play these and other roles. It has managed to remain central to our democracy and to evolve as our society has, so that there is now a broader notion of who can serve and how active the juror can be in that role.

The jury continues to reassure the parties and the larger community that verdicts in the most contested cases—the ones for which there are no clear answers—will be decided by a group of citizens who will bring their common-sense judgment to the case. The jury, in which ordinary citizens with no stake in the outcome come together temporarily to reach consensus through deliberation, continues to enjoy widespread support so much so that even when members of the larger community disagree with the jury's verdict, they accept it because they agree with the jury process by which it was reached.

As Tocqueville so presciently observed about the jury process almost 170 years ago: "The jury is both the most effective way of establishing the people's rule and the most efficient way of teaching them how to rule."[12] His words are as true today as when he wrote them.

12. TOCQUEVILLE, *supra* note 7 (Ch. 2), at 276.

*

TABLE OF CASES

References are to Pages.

---

*

INDEX

References are to pages.

273

†